Officiating Weddings

Start a Profitable Business Marrying Couples

Dayna Reid

Copyright © 2015, 2019 by Dayna Reid

Cover design by Dayna Reid
Cover image: iStockPhoto, Royalty Free
Typography by Dayna Reid

All rights reserved.
No part of this book may be reproduced in any form or by any electronic or mechanical means including information storage and retrieval systems, without permission in writing from the author. The only exception is by a reviewer, who may quote short excerpts in a review.

Printed in the United States of America
First published in eBook format: 2015
First Printing: Jan 2019

**Visit the author's website at
www.DaynaJo.com**

CONTENTS

INTRODUCTION 1

WHO CAN PERFORM THE WEDDING CEREMONY? . 3

CONSIDERATIONS FOR OFFERING OFFICIANT SERVICES 5

    WHAT IS YOUR EXPERIENCE AS AN OFFICIANT? 6
    WHAT IS YOUR SPIRITUAL OR RELIGIOUS PERSPECTIVE? 6
    HOW ACCOMMODATING ARE YOU AS AN OFFICIANT? 7
    DO YOU HAVE ANY MORAL CRITERIA THAT YOU EXPECT YOUR COUPLES TO MEET? 7
    WILL YOU OFFER PREMARITAL COUNSELING? 8
    HOW MANY MEETINGS WILL YOU PROVIDE? 8
    WILL YOU RUN THE REHEARSAL? 9
    WHAT WILL YOU WEAR? 9
    WHAT CEREMONY CHOICES WILL YOU OFFER? 10
    WILL YOU FOCUS ON SERVING? 10

PREPARATION 13

    LEARN FROM OTHERS 13
    PUBLIC SPEAKING AND TRAINING 14
    ESTABLISHING YOUR BUSINESS 14
    BUILD YOUR BUSINESS PRESENCE 15

GETTING THE WORD OUT (ADVERTISING/MARKETING) 17

    PARTICIPATE IN SOCIAL MEDIA 18
    ESTABLISH VENDOR ACCOUNTS ON WEDDING WEBSITES 19
    VENUES AND WEDDING PLANNERS 19
    ADVERTISING 20

MEETING WITH THE COUPLE 21

    INITIAL CONSULTATION AND FOLLOW-UP MEETINGS 21
    REHEARSAL DINNER AND RECEPTION ATTENDANCE 23

BACKUP PLAN 24

CREATING THE WEDDING CEREMONY SCRIPT..... 27

WEDDING CEREMONY OVERVIEW 27
PROVIDING A CEREMONY FOR YOUR COUPLES 28

COORDINATING AND CONDUCTING THE REHEARSAL 31

PREPARATION FOR THE REHEARSAL 33
ARRIVAL AT THE REHEARSAL 34
TRADITIONAL ORDER OF WEDDING PARTY AT THE ALTAR. 34
TRADITIONAL ORDER OF THE PROCESSIONAL 35
AT THE ALTAR 36
TRADITIONAL ORDER OF THE RECESSIONAL 37
ADDITIONAL CEREMONY CONSIDERATIONS: 38

OFFICIATING THE CEREMONY ON THE WEDDING DAY 39

ARRIVAL ON THE WEDDING DAY 39
PROVIDE A CALM PRESENCE 40
FAMILY DYNAMICS 41
THE CEREMONY 43

PROVIDING PRE-MARITAL COUNSELING 45

PAYMENT FOR COUNSELING SESSIONS 48

MAKING IT LEGAL 49

BECOMING AN OFFICIANT 49
ABOUT THE MARRIAGE LICENSE 51
MARRIAGE LICENSE LAWS IN THE US 52
FILING THE PAPERWORK 52

GETTING PAID 55

PRICING YOUR OFFICIANT SERVICES 55
COLLECTING THE PAYMENT 57

AFTER THE WEDDING FOLLOWING UP WITH THE COUPLE 59

ABOUT THE AUTHOR 61

Introduction

It's easy to become ordained to officiate a wedding in the United States and there is a growing trend of couples having a friend or family member get credentials online and perform their wedding ceremony. While this can result in a beautiful heartfelt ceremony delivered by someone the couple is close to, this can also be a nightmare if the newly ordained Officiant is uncomfortable speaking in front of an audience or doesn't take the time to put together a meaningful ceremony, and instead decides to "wing it."

However, you can offer a service that sets you apart from other officiants and get paid for it.

While you have access to the same online method to become ordained, you can provide a superior Officiant service to couples, which assures them—based on your established reputation—that you reliably create and deliver heartfelt wedding ceremonies with consistency and professionalism.

This book will walk you through all the steps needed to establish yourself as a reputable, well paid and in-demand Officiant.

Let's get started ...

Who Can Perform the Wedding Ceremony?

Most states in the US recognize licensed or ordained ministers, officiants, clergymen, priests, rabbis, pastors, judges and justices of the peace as authorized to perform marriage ceremonies. In some states government officials may be authorized to legally perform the ceremony.

Contrary to some popular beliefs, no state currently authorizes ship captains to perform marriages.

Each state has its own criteria for who can legally perform a marriage ceremony. The following reference is a website that lists the criteria by state, but it is still recommended that you confirm with the County Clerk in the state where the wedding will take place to verify the current requirements.

Criteria by State:

http://www.themonastery.org/wedding-laws

If you are not currently ordained, there are organizations that ordain ministers either online or through the mail (see "Becoming an Officiant" section of this book).

Considerations for Offering Officiant Services

It is important to match the services you offer as an Officiant (also known as "Minister") to the needs of the couple you have agreed to marry. If you are unable or unwilling to carry out the desires of the couple, then you need to clearly communicate this from the beginning. The words spoken at the ceremony should reflect what the couple believes and feels. Here are some considerations when offering your services as an Officiant.

What is your experience as an Officiant?

The government does not issue licenses to ministers, so an Officiant's experience with weddings is important. How many weddings have you performed? Do you have references the couple can contact? Do you have credentials you can show to the couple? If you are brand new to officiating, you could initially offer your services for free and let the couples know that you are donating your time to gain expertise. Many couples will be happy to have you officiate for free. Then, once you have done several ceremonies, you could begin to charge a small fee and gradually increase it as your experience increases.

What is your spiritual or religious perspective?

Many ministers subscribe to the doctrines of a particular faith. If you have specific religious values that could interfere with the beliefs of the couple, let them know this in the first meeting. Can you work with them to create a ceremony that is true to their beliefs, or do you feel uncomfortable with their particular denominational preferences? Will you be able to work well with their beliefs?

How accommodating are you as an Officiant?

If the couple wants a non-traditional song played during the ceremony, will you allow it? Are you okay with the couple adding their own vows or other special, romantic touches? If the couple wants a little humor in the ceremony, would you feel comfortable accommodating them? Will you allow for changes as the wedding day approaches? Will you allow flash photography during the wedding? Will you work with the couple to develop a ceremony which honors their religious or non-religious traditions and beliefs?

Do you have any moral criteria that you expect your couples to meet?

If the couple is living together, already has children, is expecting a child, or if either of them has been through a divorce, would these or other circumstances be an issue for you? If so, it is important to ask the necessary questions in your first conversation to identify any areas of concern for you and either set expectations with the couple to alleviate your concerns or decline providing the service. If you are uncomfortable in any way with providing the service, it is best the couple find someone better suited to their needs.

Will you offer premarital counseling?

Some couples want counseling, and others don't feel it's necessary. Will you offer this as a service? If you receive your ordination through seminary, you will likely obtain the training necessary to offer this service. If not, there are other organizations, like, "Prepare/Enrich" which can provide the education needed for you to offer counseling to your couples (see the "Premarital Counseling" section of this book for more information).

How many meetings will you provide?

Will you say no meeting is necessary and just show up for the wedding and let the couple run their own rehearsal? Will you offer one or two preparatory meetings and a rehearsal? Can you meet the couple's wishes for frequency and method of interaction? Will you be available to talk by phone as questions arise? What is your preferred method of working with the couple to create their ceremony? Are you willing to meet in person, or will you only work with them over the phone or via email?

Will you run the rehearsal?

An experienced Officiant at the wedding rehearsal can be very helpful. If you are unable or unwilling to attend the rehearsal, will other arrangements be made for someone to lead the wedding party through the steps? For more elaborate weddings, it is important to have someone available to guide the couple and their attendants through the practice of the ceremony, so that they know what to expect.

What will you wear?

Some Officiants wear suits (a black suit is desirable as it blends in with any color scheme), some wear robes, and others wear a wide variety of garments from jeans and tennis shoes to butterfly wings (yes, someone actually showed up to perform a ceremony wearing butterfly wings)! What will you wear? If it is too ornate, or if it has prominent religious symbols, which may offend some family members, you will want to ask the couple if your choice is acceptable for them.

What ceremony choices will you offer?

Many officiants have only one ceremony they offer. If you plan to offer only a one or two ceremony options to your couples, be sure you let them review the ceremony to ensure that it expresses what they want communicated at their wedding. Will you have any spontaneous words that you will add to the ceremony? Some officiants will have a few simple ceremony choices with the option for the couple to add some personalized ideas. Others will design an elaborate, customized wedding just for them.

Will you focus on serving?

Many people feel that they have to meet a minister's (or "Officiant") standards, and in some religious traditions this is entirely valid. But remember, the original meaning of the word "minister" is "servant." Are you willing to meet the needs of the couple on their big day? Are they comfortable in your presence, or do they feel like they have to withhold things to prevent your disapproval? Do they feel pressured to behave differently to gain your approval? The best Officiant is one who is eager to serve and make the couple's wedding day a beautiful one for everyone.

Preparation

Now it's time to lay the groundwork for offering your services for pay.

Learn From Others

You may want to start by attending a few weddings to learn how others officiate. Take note of their style, their words, their approachability, etc. Think about how you would like to provide your service—would it be similar or different from what you observe?

Public Speaking and Training

Are you at ease speaking in front of an audience? If not, you may want to pursue training in public speaking, or join a Toastmasters group in your area. Are you comfortable with taking the material presented in this book and venturing out on your own, or do you prefer more formal training? There are several organizations that offer Celebrant training to teach you how to conduct a wedding ceremony. Or, if you're like me, you can gather the information you need and offer your first few weddings for free to perfect your process.

Establishing Your Business

Obtain a license to do business from your state. Each state has its own process and fees for establishing your company. The U.S. Small Business Administration website is a good resource for determining what is needed in your state:

Website for the U.S. Small Business Administration: https://www.sba.gov

Build Your Business Presence

Before you have your first meeting with a client, you will want to have a few things in place for them to feel like you are legitimate.

Establish Your Physical Location – If you are operating your business out of your home, but meeting with clients elsewhere, you may not want your personal address to be made public (especially on the Internet). Rather than publicize your home address, you can rent a post office box and use the PO Box address on all your business correspondence, your website, and your business cards.

Create a Website – Having a professionally designed website promotes confidence in your clients that the service you provide is an established and legitimate business. There are many free or low-cost options for building your own website with minimal technical skill. However, if you want something more professional looking, you will need to hire someone to create one for you. If you don't know anyone personally to help you with this, there is a great online resource for finding someone to do it for minimal cost. On this website you will post your project and people with the expertise you need will bid on it (and each person who bids will have reviews and other statistics available for you to make the best choice).

Website for hiring a professional for your project: http://www.upwork.com

Obtain Business Cards – When meeting with new clients you will want to have business cards you can leave with them for contacting you later. These cards can also be given to people at networking events to gain new clients.

Getting the Word Out (Advertising/Marketing)

So, how will people find you? How will they know that you provide Officiant Services? There are many options for creating this awareness. Some options cost money and others don't. As mentioned earlier, first establish a business website. This will provide a place for potential clients to obtain additional information about the service you provide and give you a link to share with other established wedding websites to promote your business.

Participate in Social Media

There are many social media options available for promoting your business. Keep in mind when communicating in this arena it is more important to make friends than to "sell" your services. If you do a good job of being kind and helpful, your service will sell itself. People want to work with people that they like.

The two main social media tools I recommend are Facebook and Twitter. Create a Facebook page for your business to engage with couples and other wedding vendors. This is a great place to network with people who will refer you if they like you. Create a Twitter account and link your Facebook page to it and automatically tweet your Facebook posts.

Once again, remember to engage with your audience. Post information that is relevant and helpful to your Facebook and Twitter community. Answer questions promptly and kindly. Be generous with your time and information.

Establish Vendor Accounts on Wedding Websites

Two of the main wedding websites for establishing a professional presence are WeddingWire.com and TheKnot.com. Both of these sites have paid account (range: $40-$200 a month) and free account options. With a paid account you are much more visible—typically featured within a short list of other officiants. With a free account you are somewhat lost in a long list of other Officiants with free accounts. But it is still a way to link your website to another reputable wedding website. Also, both of these sites (even with a free account) have easy-to-use tools for requesting reviews from your clients and then displaying those reviews to prospective clients.

Venues and Wedding Planners

Another way of getting new wedding business is to work with venues and wedding planners. Reach out to the wedding venues in your area, give them your card and if they like you they will refer you to their couples who come to them to book their wedding venue. Similarly, with wedding planners, reach out to them, ask them to coffee, tell them what your philosophy is, and the service you provide to couples and if they like you, they will refer you.

Advertising

There are many options for paid advertising: wedding magazines, ads on wedding websites, Google ads, Facebook ads, etc. The ads are usually expensive and result in limited or no benefit. Instead, I recommend posting an ad on Craigslist.org for free. With a Craigslist ad, you can include pictures of your logo and previous weddings you've performed, as well as provide a link to your website for more information.

Meeting With the Couple

Initial consultation and follow-up meetings

The initial meeting can take place anywhere you choose and usually lasts 30-60 minutes. I prefer to meet with the couple at a coffee shop, in a location half the distance between where we both live. The first meeting is any opportunity for the three of you to meet in person and determine if you would work well together.

When the couple arrives for the meeting, introduce yourself, give them a business card, and ask them how they met and how they became engaged. Spend a little time getting to know them. Next, provide them with an overview your services and the process you will follow to work with them on their ceremony and officiate on their wedding day. You can also give them a document that outlines some of this information to take with them to review later.

If the couple decides during the first meeting to hire you as their Officiant, make sure you collect all the details you will need to create and officiate their ceremony. If you have a couple of ceremonies that you use, you will allow them to select which one they want to use. If you plan to customize their ceremony, give them any resources (documents you've created or a book with ceremony selections, etc.) you have chosen to help facilitate this process. I give my clients my book, "*Do-It-Yourself Wedding Ceremony: Choosing the Perfect Words and Officiating Your Unforgettable Day*" to use for creating their personalized ceremony (the cost for the book is built into my Officiant fee). I have them read through the book and select all the wording choices that they like and then I put together the draft of the ceremony script for their approval. But you can provide any resources to your couples that work for you.

Once they have chosen you to preside over their special day, you will want to let them know your preferred method of communication for working on their ceremony and answering any questions they may have. Maybe you only want to communicate via phone or email after the initial meeting. Or maybe you prefer face-to-face. I don't have a preference so I leave it up to the couple to decide whether they want to meet in person, communicate by telephone, email or video conference (like "Skype").

Rehearsal dinner and reception attendance

Some couples may want you to attend the rehearsal dinner or reception, or both. One of the benefits of attending the rehearsal dinner is that it gives you an opportunity to get to know the wedding party better, so that on the wedding day, you are more like one of the family and less of a stranger. This puts everyone at ease and makes them more likely to reach out to you with any questions or concerns.

Rather than make my attendance at these events a required part of my service, I offer it as an option, and I let them know that there is no obligation to invite me—that it is completely up to them. But I also let them know that if they want me to attend, I would love to.

You will need to decide what works best for you as an Officiant. Maybe you offer to attend the rehearsal dinner, but decline the reception invitation. Whatever you decide, make sure you communicate your availability or unavailability to your clients.

Backup Plan

Besides the couple, you are the most important member of the wedding party. If you don't show up, they cannot get married. Therefore, it is vital that you have someone you can call to perform the ceremony if you become ill or have a family emergency and can't be there. Network with other Officiants to find people you trust to be there for you in case you are unexpectedly unavailable.

Creating the Wedding Ceremony Script

Wedding Ceremony Overview

There are many elements to choose from when creating your ceremony, but there are only two elements that are legally required: the Declaration of Intent and the pronouncement of marriage. In other words, you could literally have a ceremony that read: "Chris, do you agree to marry John? And John, do you agree to marry Chris? I now pronounce you married." All other elements are optional, which gives you tremendous flexibility in designing a ceremony that is the most meaningful to the couple.

In addition to the basic elements of a traditional ceremony, there are several other special touches that can be added to the ceremony to make it unique and personal for the couple, such as including children, honoring parents or grandparents, remembering loved ones that are unable to attend or have passed on, etc.

Providing a Ceremony for Your Couples

You can plan to work with each couple to fully customize their ceremony, or simply offer one or more pre-written options. My book, "*Do-It-Yourself Wedding Ceremony: Choosing the Perfect Words and Officiating Your Unforgettable Day*" is a great resource for helping you to build a wedding ceremony from beginning to end. This book contains everything you need to create and personalize wedding ceremonies as well as provides several complete sample ceremonies from which your couples choose.

Link to Wedding Ceremony Book:
http://www.amazon.com/Do-Yourself-Wedding-Ceremony-Unforgettable-ebook/dp/B00L3SWX0S/

Coordinating and Conducting the Rehearsal

If the couple has more than one attendant on each side, or they are including any additional elements, like a candle lighting or sand ceremony, then it's beneficial to do a rehearsal of the wedding ceremony.

The average duration of a wedding ceremony is approximately 20 minutes. Practicing the steps ahead of time gives everyone a chance to understand what to expect and what is expected of them. This can alleviate the wedding party's fear of the unknown and ease their anxiety of being in front of an audience.

Typically the rehearsal will take place at the location of the ceremony and be coordinated by either the venue coordinator or wedding planner. The Officiant will attend the rehearsal and assist with practicing the logistics (handling of the rings, lighting candles, etc.) of the ceremony that takes place once the couple arrives at the altar. When no one else is available to lead the rehearsal, then the Officiant can fill this role and coordinate the entire run-through.

You will want to walk through the rehearsal at least two times to make sure everyone is comfortable with his or her role. The goal is to practice until the wedding party feels confident that they can do what is expected of them on the wedding day.

Preparation for the rehearsal

Prior to the rehearsal, you will want to gather all the information necessary to conduct the practice in the most efficient way. Many venues limit you to one hour for use of their facility to perform your practice activities. So, you will want to make the most of this time by being prepared.

Here is some information to gather in advance:

- Who will conduct the rehearsal?
- Where will the rehearsal be conducted? Date? Time?
- Is parking provided? If so, where?
- Will there be candle lighting, readings, etc., requiring additional coordination?
- If there is a rehearsal dinner, have you been asked to attend?
- Are there any commuting considerations for the date/time of the rehearsal? For example, should you arrive early to avoid getting stuck in rush-hour traffic?

Arrival at the Rehearsal

When you arrive at the rehearsal location, you will want to collect the final payment for your services to avoid handling money on the wedding day and review the marriage license paperwork. Make sure that all the fields on the form are completed with the exception of the signatures. The document will be signed after the wedding ceremony. You can either give the form back to the couple, or offer to hold on to it for them until the ceremony.

Traditional order of wedding party at the altar

There are many ways to conduct a rehearsal, but I prefer to start with everyone taking their place at the altar so they know their destination for the processional. To begin the wedding rehearsal, have everyone line up at the altar in the order they will be standing during the ceremony. Traditionally, the Officiant stands facing the guests. The groom stands to the left of the Officiant and the best man stands to his left, followed by the groomsmen. The bride stands to the right of the Officiant and the maid or matron of honor stands to the right of the bride, followed by the bridesmaids.

If there are ring bearers or flower girls, depending on their age, they will either stand in front of the groomsmen/bridesmaids at the altar or they will be seated in the front row with an adult once their job has been completed.

Traditional order of the processional

The walk-down-the-aisle, also known as the processional, can begin with the groom and Officiant (as well as the best man and possibly the groomsmen) already at the altar, or they can walk with the rest of the wedding party.

If everyone in the wedding party is going to walk, then the Officiant will walk first to indicate to the guests that the ceremony is officially beginning. The groom then escorts his mother, or mother and father together, to their seats and then joins the Officiant at the altar. If the groom is escorting his mother, then the couple may want to have someone escort the bride's mother as well.

The bridesmaids walk either alone or escorted by groomsmen. If escorted, then the bridesmaids and groomsmen will separate at the front of the altar and take their places, in order of furthest from the couple to closest to the couple—finishing with the best man and maid or matron of honor going last and standing closest to the couple.

Next, the ring bearer walks with the flower girl or is followed by the flower girl, who will drop flower petals along the path that the bride will follow.

Finally, the bride is escorted down the aisle by her father (or other family member or friend). When she is at the front of the altar, the groom takes a few steps forward to greet her. The bride hugs her dad, or whoever escorts her. The groom shakes the escort's hand, or can hug him or her, and then the bride's escort places the bride's hand in the groom's hand so he can escort her to the altar. The bride then hands her bouquet to her maid or matron of honor.

At the altar

The bride and groom face each other in front of the Officiant.

With everyone at the altar, you can run through the logistics of the ceremony. You won't perform the ceremony, but you will share any cues that will be given to indicate someone will be expected to do something. For example, you may let everyone know that after the couple exchanges their vows, you will say, "The rings please," and that the person who has the rings (typically the best man) will come forward and give them to the couple for the ring exchange. Or if there will be a candle lighting ceremony, this would be the time to determine where the candles will be and if the taper candles used to light the unity candle will be pre-lit and who will perform this task. This is also the time to determine where and when the couple would like to sign the marriage license. Signing can be done as part of the ceremony, or done immediately after the ceremony.

Traditional order of the recessional

The walk-back-down-the-aisle after the ceremony, also known as the recessional, begins at the end of the wedding ceremony. This is usually indicated by the presentation of the couple as husband and wife or after the kiss. The wedding party will exit the altar the opposite of the way they came in. The bride and groom will go first, followed by the best man and maid or matron of honor, followed by the bridesmaids and groomsmen, etc. The Officiant exits last, followed by the parents who were escorted into the ceremony.

Additional ceremony considerations:

- The groomsmen can act as ushers for seating the guests prior to the ceremony.
- If the ring bearer is a child, the best man can carry the actual rings and the child can carry decorative rings for the ceremony.
- Determine who will cue the start of the ceremony.
- Determine who will be the two witnesses for signing the marriage license.

Officiating the Ceremony on the Wedding Day

Arrival on the wedding day

To give yourself time to address any last-minute issues and to put the couple's minds at ease, plan to arrive at the ceremony location at least one hour prior to the start of the wedding. As soon as you arrive, let someone in the wedding party know that you are there and to let the couple know that you have arrived. If you do not have the marriage license yet, request it. You will want to review the form to make sure all the fields have been filled in with the exception of the signatures. If you have not collected payment yet, you will need to locate the appropriate person and collect it (preferably when you first arrive, rather than after the ceremony). If the couple is writing their own vows, and they have not given a copy of them to you yet, now is the time to ask for them, so that you can give the vows to them at the appropriate time during the ceremony. If there are any props needed for additional elements of the ceremony, such as candles for a candle lighting ceremony, make sure that they are in place and ready to go for the wedding.

Provide a calm presence

In addition to your job of officiating the wedding, your primary focus is to be a calming presence for the wedding party. Many people are anxious about being in front of an audience, and some can become so nervous that they collapse. You can prevent this by paying attention to the body language of the people in the wedding, especially the couple you are marrying. Pay close attention to any signs of distress. If one of them looks uneasy, or if they have told you they are nervous, ask him or her to take a couple of deep breaths and suggest they relax their knees (especially at the altar). If the ceremony hasn't started yet, you can distract the person from their tension by asking them questions about anything other than the ceremony—"So, how about those Seahawks?"

Family dynamics

For a variety of reasons, families have members who don't get along well. Maybe a parent feels slighted by being left out of something, or one of the mothers dreads seeing her ex-husband with his much younger wife. Whatever the case may be, these grievances can sometimes interfere with the couple's wedding day. For example, if one of the family members has made it known that they will not attend the wedding if so-and-so is there, or that they want to be kept far away from that person if they do attend, then this situation could present drama on the wedding day.

As the Officiant, you can play a key role in providing a calm presence and running interference before any issues escalate. If the couple has communicated with you that someone in their family could be a potential problem, you can assure them that you will locate the person on the wedding day and that you will keep an eye on them and distract them from whatever disagreements they are fixated on.

When you arrive for the ceremony, have the couple identify the person of concern, then carefully observe them. Do they look relaxed or tense? Are they having a contentious conversation with someone? If you see any trouble brewing, make it your job to get them focused on themselves, rather than their discontent. Pull them aside and remind them of the role they are playing at the wedding and that their main job is to support the couple on one of the most important days of their lives. Explain how significant they are to that process and how happy the couple is that they are there and able to participate in this occasion. Tell them, "You don't want to be remembered as anything other than loving and supportive on this day."

The key to success in handling difficult dynamics is to keep the focus where it belongs: on the couple and their special day.

The ceremony

Once the ceremony has begun, to prevent unexpected and undesirable results, don't deviate from the wedding script. Your idea of a joke may not seem so funny to several close family members or your spontaneous inclusion of a religious prayer may not be well received by your atheist couple. During the ceremony, it is best to speak only the words that have been previously approved by the couple, unless they have specifically asked you to say something spontaneously, like a prayer.

Also, make sure you pronounce names correctly. You can stick a post-it note to the wedding script with the phonetic pronunciation of any difficult names.

When it comes to the "repeat-after-me" part of the ceremony, be sure to give them the words to speak in eight or less syllabic phrases. This will help prevent you from having to repeat phrases multiple times and having them forget what you've said, which can cause them embarrassment.

If the signing of the marriage license was not part of the wedding ceremony, at the conclusion of the ceremony, you will make your way, along with the couple and their two witnesses, to the pre-designated area to sign the document.

Once the documents have been signed, you can ask to take a photograph with the couple for your records and keep the photo along with copies of all their paperwork in your files. You may also want to give them a keepsake copy of their wedding ceremony script to remember their special day. In the footer of the pages of the script you can include your contact information for future referrals.

Providing Pre-marital Counseling

There are many ways to structure and offer pre-marital counseling to your couples. This chapter will cover the way that has worked for me, based on the Prepare/Enrich Pre-marital Counseling curriculum. But, keep in mind that this is not the only option.

Here is the link for more information on Prepare/Enrich training: http://www.prepare-enrich.com

Once you have acquired the necessary training, you can advertise this offering as one of your services.

The counseling begins with an online assessment. Through the Prepare/Enrich website a separate link to the questionnaire will be sent to each individual. Prepare/Enrich will notify you once both people have completed it.

The items the couple will respond to are based on research and are intended to help them identify the unique strengths and potential growth areas of their premarital relationship.

Some relationship areas that the questionnaire assesses are:

- Communication
- Conflict resolution
- Roles
- Sexuality and Affection
- Finances
- Spiritual beliefs
- Children and Parenting

Once you have reviewed the couple's report (provide by Prepare/Enrich), based on the online assessment, you will meet with the couple to provide feedback by helping them understand their results and learn important relationship skills. In the first meeting with the couple, following the assessment, you will determine how many additional sessions may be needed to follow up on any possible growth areas.

Subsequent meetings will consist of addressing any specific growth areas that were identified in the assessment. In these meetings, through conversation and exercises, you may explore individual personality traits, compare family backgrounds and how the differences may affect the relationship, work on—strengthening communication skills, resolving conflicts and reducing stress, comfortably discussing financial issues, as well as establishing personal, couple, and family goals.

The Marriage Builders website is another great resource for finding free tools to use in your counseling sessions. The "Questionnaires" page has an "Emotional Needs Questionnaire" that is especially helpful in working with couples.

Here is the link to the Marriage Builders website:

http://www.marriagebuilders.com//graphic/mbi4500_resource.html

Payment for counseling sessions

Prepare/Enrich charges you a fee for each couple's online questionnaire, so you will want to factor that into the price you set for the assessment and initial meeting (approximately one hour) with the couple. You can then set an hourly rate for any subsequent meetings.

Making it Legal

Becoming an Officiant

An Officiant is someone who performs a religious rite or presides over a religious service or ceremony. It is simply another word for Clergy or Minister and commonly used to refer to people authorized to perform marriage ceremonies, especially for non-denominational and non-religious ceremonies.

The United States in general does not attempt to define what an organization must be in order to qualify as a church or what qualifications are necessary to be a minister. This goes back to early American history and the separation of Church and State. Each religious denomination has its own requirements for becoming ordained.

If you wish to become ordained and are not affiliated with a particular religious denomination, there are several religious organizations in the U.S. that provide non-denominational ordination (no training necessary; sometimes a fee is charged). One of these organizations is Universal Life Church. By visiting their website and completing a form online, a person can become ordained for free with the click of a button.

Website for Universal Life Church:
http://www.themonastery.org/

Some states require you to either register a Letter of Good Standing or a Copy of your credentials at the County courthouse. Other states require you to request and file an application. It is recommended that you verify the requirements for the state where the ceremony will take place with the County

Clerk prior to performing a marriage ceremony.

For information on Officiant requirements by state:

http://www.themonastery.org/wedding-laws

About the Marriage License

What are the differences between the marriage license and the marriage certificate? The marriage *license* is a legal document, obtained by the couple, that authorizes a designated party to perform the ceremony, allowing them to get married; the marriage *certificate* is the form filed with the state which officially certifies that the nuptials took place and once recorded is the official document that proves they are married (a certified copy may be requested from the state once the marriage has been recorded).

Marriage License Laws in the US

Each state has specific marriage license laws for a couple to wed. Although there are differences between the requirements in the various states, a marriage performed in one state must be recognized by every other state under the Full Faith and Credit Clause of the United States Constitution. The following reference is a website that lists the criteria by state, but it is still recommended that you confirm with the state where the wedding will take place to verify their current requirements.

For information on Marriage License Laws by state: http://usmarriagelaws.com/

Filing the Paperwork

The couple receives the appropriate documents when they apply for their marriage license. The couple then provides the you, the Officiant, with the marriage license and marriage certificate documents prior to the wedding ceremony. A portion of the marriage certificate form will be completed by the couple in advance of the ceremony and the rest of it will be completed after the ceremony (i.e. signing the document and completing the Officiant information).

After the marriage ceremony is performed, you have the duty of sending a copy of the marriage certificate to the county or state agency that records marriage certificates. The couple may then request a certified copy of the certificate from the county or state agency once the marriage has been recorded. Some Officiants will order a certified copy for the couple as an added service at the time they send in the paperwork.

Failure to send the marriage certificate to the appropriate agency does not necessarily nullify the marriage, but it may make proof of the marriage more difficult.

Getting Paid

Pricing your Officiant services

When determining how much to charge for your Officiant services, you will want to take into consideration your level of experience. How many weddings have your performed? As you gain experience, and begin to receive referrals from other couples, you can increase your fee. But initially, you may want to offer your service for free, especially for the first couple of weddings, to build your self-confidence and fine-tune your process.

Check with wedding planners and other Officiants to determine what the average rate is for officiating in your region, which will dictate a price range. If you price yourself too low (which is acceptable when you are establishing your business) some may think you have no experience or are unprofessional. If you price yourself too high then you will probably attract a limited number of potential clients.

If you are near a big city, the price range for your type of service will likely be higher than if you are in an area hundreds of miles away from a large city. Because the cost-of-living is different in each location, the fee you can successfully charge will be different in each area also.

When setting prices for your services, you can either establish a fixed price, which includes all the services you offer (wedding, rehearsal, travel costs within a specified radius, etc.), regardless of whether or not the couple takes advantage of them all. Alternatively, you can create a menu of services and charge individually for each service. You, can also set your rates using a combination of flat rate pricing with add-on costs for things like gasoline for extra travel outside your indicated area, or an extra charge for rehearsal attendance.

Collecting the payment

Whichever method you choose, collect a non-refundable deposit to secure the wedding date at the time of the booking. This amount should be at least fifteen percent of the total cost of the services booked to offset the loss of business if the couple should cancel. Then require that the remaining balance due be paid at the rehearsal. This will prevent you from having to have a conversation about money or handling money on the wedding day, when your focus should be solely on the sacredness of the ceremony.

After the Wedding Following Up With the Couple

Your role as an Officiant is significant in the lives of those you marry. You have established a relationship that they will not soon forget. It is up to you to stay in touch and keep the quality services you provided fresh in their minds for referring you to future clients.

Once the wedding day is over, and a couple of weeks have gone by, you can reach out to the couple and request a review of your services. There are several free online options for collecting reviews (Yelp, Wedding Wire, The Knot, etc.) that you can use. Most of these sites have the tools you need to set up a customized email that you then request to be sent to the couple so that they can post a review. You can then include a link to these reviews on your business website for potential clients to see.

On the couple's one-year anniversary, you can send them a card, wishing them a "Happy Anniversary" to let them know you are thinking of them on this special day, and also include your contact information for future business.

About the Author

Dayna Reid, Bestselling Author, Writer, and Minister. She has officiated weddings for over 17 years. Her love for people and the desire to provide couples with a non-judgmental and personalized approach to selecting the words spoken at their wedding inspired her to seek ministry ordination. Although Dayna personally believes in God, she also believes that "everyone has to find their own way in this world, including any beliefs they may have about the mysteries. Because truly, all we really have is a faith in what we believe to be true."

Amazon Bestseller

Do-It-Yourself Wedding Ceremony

Choosing the Perfect Words and Officiating Your Unforgettable Day

Dayna Reid's third edition of the book "Do-It-Yourself Wedding Ceremony" includes: Step-by-step, informative chapters, which describe the elements of a wedding ceremony from beginning to end, and the choices people can make with each element. "<u>Do-It-Yourself Wedding Ceremony</u>" includes a wealth of wording and ceremony selections, to celebrate diverse styles, beliefs and traditions, from Christian to Zen, to the simple declarations of love that transcend tradition.

Available at Amazon.com, BarnesandNoble.com, and wherever books are sold

Made in the USA
Coppell, TX
28 August 2024

A Complete User Guide to the iPhone 12 mini

A step by step guide to Your iPhone 12 mini

Bernard Gates

copyright@2020

TABLE OF CONTENT

Introduction 14

Chapter 1: Setting up your new iPhone 12 mini 15

   Moving Data and Stuff from A Previous Phone 15

   How to Set Up iPhone 12 mini As A New Phone 18

   Moving Data from an Android Device 19

   Moving Data To Your iPhone VIA iCloud 23

   Transferring Your Data via the macOS Catalina Option 24

   Moving your data via macOS Mojave and older 27

Chapter 2: The Face ID 30

   Setting up the Face ID on the iphone 12 mini 30

   Turning Off Require Attention for Face ID 31

   Resetting Face ID 32

   Adding a second Face to Face ID 32

   Using Face ID to Unlock, Apple Pay, App Store Purchases etc 33

   Managing Face ID Use with Apps 34

   Managing Attention Features for Face ID 34

   Disabling Face ID Temporarily 35

Chapter 3: Setting up "Hey Siri" 36

   Using "Hey siri" 37

Chapter 4: Setting up Apple ID 38

   Creating an Apple ID 38

   Signing In to iCloud With an Existing Apple ID 40

   Signing Out of iCloud 40

Chapter 5: Setting up Apple Pay 42

   Changing the Initial Card for Apple Pay 44

Removing a Card from Apple Pay 45

Chapter 6: Setting up and using the haptic touch 46

Rearranging or deleting Apps on the Home screen with Haptic touch 46

Widgets 46

Using Haptic Touch with Notifications 47

Customizing the Haptic Touch 48

Chapter 7: iOS 14 features and functions 50

Moving Widgets to the Home Screen from Today View 50

Adding a Widget to a Home Screen Page 50

Editing a Widget 51

Removing a widget from the Home Screen 51

Viewing the Today View from your Lock screen 51

Using the App Library 51

Adding new Apps from the App store to the Home screen and App Library or App Library Only 52

Hiding and Showing Home Screen Pages 52

App Clips 52

Getting and using an App Clip 52

Using the Translate App 53

Translating a Conversation 54

Downloading Languages for Offline Translation 55

Using the Search Function 55

Searching in Apps 56

Using the picture in picture function 56

Messages: pinning a Conversation 57

Switching from a Messages conversation to FaceTime or Audio Call 57

Mentioning people in a conversation 58

Replying to a Specific Message in a Conversation 58

Designing your very own Memoji... 59

Using the Health App to set up Sleep Schedules 60

Making Changes to your next Alarm... 61

Changing or adding a sleep schedule... 61

Changing your Wind Down Schedule and Activity 62

Using the Health Checklist Function to Manage Health Features 62

Chapter 8: Setting Up and Using the Control Center ... 63

How to Open the Control Center on Your Device 63

Adding Controls to the Control Center 63

Organizing the Hierarchy of Controls in the Control Center 64

Removing Controls from the Control Center 65

Disabling Control Center on the Lock Screen..................................... 65

Disabling the Control Center from Apps... 66

Chapter 9: Adjusting settings 67

Making Text Bolder and Bigger.. 67

Changing the Text Buttons... 67

Reducing the White Point... 68

Deactivating Parallax and App Zooms 68

Turning off the Lower-case Keyboard 69

Enabling Character Preview... 70

Turning off Reachability.. 71

Disabling" Shake to undo" 71

3

Adjusting the Audio and Information Settings 71

Adjusting the Maps Navigation Volume 72

Siri Settings 72

Controlling Siri's Voice Feedback 73

Deactivating Siri Suggestions 73

Routing Calls Manually to Speaker or Bluetooth 74

Chapter 10: Taking a screen shot with your iPhone 76

How to take a Screen Shot: 76

Viewing and Editing Screen Shots 76

Taking a Screen Shot Using the Assistive Touch Capability of the iphone 12 mini 77

Chapter 11: Sim settings and operation 79

Setting Up Your Cellular Plan 79

To Scan a QR Code 79

Using a service provider App 80

Entering SIM Information Manually 80

Switch Between SIMs 81

Erasing a SIM 81

Labelling Your Plans 82

Setting Your Default Number 82

Let Your Phone Remember the Number to Use 83

You can Switch Phone Numbers Before Making a Call with the Steps Below: 83

Follow the Steps Below to Choose a Particular Phone Number to Send a Message With: 84

Choosing the Number for Cellular Data 85

Allow Cellular Data Switching 85

Manage Cellular Settings 86

Chapter 12: iMessaging 87

Turning on "Read receipts" on or off in iMessages. 87

Turning Messages Previews on/off 88

Telling the Difference Between Sending an iMessage or an SMS/MMS 89

Sending a Text Message via iMessage 89

Sending a New Photo or Video using Messages 90

Sending an Existing Photo or Video via iMessage 91

Sending your Current Location Using iMessage 92

Sharing your Location for a Period of Time 92

Sharing a Contact Card through iMessages Via the Contacts App ... 93

Sending your Location from the Maps 94

Sending Messages via iMessage using Siri 95

Changing Which Apple ID iMessage Uses on iPhone 96

Chapter 13: Photos 98

Creating a New Album in the Photos App 98

Creating Shared Albums in the Photos App 99

Adding Photos and Videos to Existing Albums in the Photo App 101

Navigating Between Moments, Collections and Years Smart Groups 103

Moving Between Years, Months and Days 103

Viewing Picture and Video Locations on a Map 104

Quickly selecting a Month to Jump to from the Years View 105

Copying a Video or Picture to the Clipboard in Moments or Albums 105

5

Quickly Copying Pictures or Videos from Moments to the Clipboard 106

Hiding Images 107

How to Unhide Photos 108

Unhiding Photos or Albums 109

Locating Memories in Photos 111

Searching Memories 111

Taking a Photo 112

Taking a Burst shot 113

Taking a Live Photo 113

Recording a Video 113

Recording a Quick Take Video 114

Recording a Slow-Motion Video 114

Playing a Portion of Recorded Video in Slow Motion 115

Changing the Slow-Motion Recording Settings 115

Capturing a Time-Lapse Video 115

Using Quick Toggles to Change Video Resolution and Frame Rate .. 115

Setting the Flash 115

Setting the Timer 115

Switching in Between Cameras (front and rear facing) 116

How to take a Square Photo 117

How to take a Panorama 118

Enhancing Images in Photos 119

How to Enhance Photos 120

Changing Lighting with Smart Adjustments in Photos 121

Changing the lighting in your photos 123

6

Changing Color in your Photos 124

Converting Photos to Black and White 125

Fine-tuning with Smart Adjustments in Photos 127

Reverting to Original Photo 128

Trimming your video 129

Resizing a Video 130

Flipping and Rotating a Video 131

Adjusting the Video Brightness 132

Adding a Video Filter 132

Muting video Sounds 133

Using Filters in the Photos App 133

Rotating Photos 134

To Straighten Photos 136

Cropping Photos 137

Changing the Aspect Ratio in Photos 138

Turning on Photo and Video Extensions in Photos in the Photo app 138

Accessing and Using Photo and Video Extensions in the Photos app 140

Assigning Pictures to Contacts Via the Photo App 141

Using the Photo App to set Your Wall paper 142

Starting a Slideshow with the Photos App 143

Playing a Whole Album as a Slide Show 144

Airplaying Your photos to Your TV 145

Sharing Individual Photos or Videos Using Photos 146

sharing individual photos or videos 146

Sharing Multiple Photos 146

Printing Photos 147

Using Siri to Locate Photos Based on Time 149

Using Siri to Find Photos Based on Location 149

Using Siri to Find Photos of Things 150

Searching for Photos in the Photos App 150

Using the Search Bar to Find What you Want in the Photos App 151

Using Names to Make People Easier to Locate in the Photos App ... 151

Chapter 14: Music 152

Locating Songs in Music 153

To Go to Recent Searches to Locate Something: 154

Browsing for Songs in Music 154

How to Download Songs 155

To Remove Downloaded Songs from Cache 155

Deleting songs from your music library 156

Accessing playlists 156

Playing a playlist 157

Creating a New Playlist 158

Adding Tracks to a Playlist 158

Arranging Tracks on a playlist 160

Removing a Track from a Playlist 161

Deleting a playlist 161

Creating a Genius Playlist 162

Using Up Next 163

Quickly Add Music to up Next from Anywhere 163

How to Quickly clear Up Next from Anywhere 164

To view Your Up Next Queue 164

Viewing Your Up Next History ... 165

Adding music to Up Next ... 166

Re-arranging What's Up Next ... 166

Removing a Track from Up Next ... 167

Clearing Music from Up Next ... 167

Chapter 15: Mail ... 168

Setting Up Mail on Your Device ... 168

Setting Up Outlook.com Mail ... 169

Setting up Exchange Mail ... 169

Setting Up IMAP/POP, CalDav and CardDAV ... 170

Setting Up a Default Email ... 171

Switching Between Email Accounts ... 172

Disabling an Email Account ... 173

Deleting an Email Account ... 173

Getting New Mail Notifications ... 174

Managing Small Accounts ... 175

Changing Preview Lines ... 175

Displaying To/Cc Labels ... 176

Adjusting Swipe Options ... 176

How to toggle Ask Before Deleting ... 177

Loading Remote Images ... 177

Organizing Emails by Thread ... 178

Collapsing Read Messages ... 178

Moving a Thread's Most Recent Message to the Top ... 179

Turning Complete Threads on and Off ... 180

How to Turn Always Bcc Myself on and off ... 180

Marking Addresses 181

Turning Increase Quote Level on and off 181

Setting Your Signature 182

Mark an Email as Read or Unread 182

Flagging an Email 183

Adding New Mailboxes 184

Moving Messages to Different Mailboxes 185

Adding Contacts to Your VIP List 186

Filtering Inboxes in the Mail App 186

Unsubscribing to Mailing Lists 187

Creating a New Email in the Mail App 188

Choosing an Email Address from Your Contacts in the Mail App 189

How to Access Drafts in the Mail App 190

Using Siri to Send Email 190

Making Siri Read Your Unread Emails 191

Asking Siri to Respond to an Email 192

Using Siri to Create a Contact Relationship 193

Adding a New Email Address to a Contact in the Mail App 193

Inserting a Photo or Video into an Email in the Mail App 194

Adding an Attachment to a Mail 196

Saving a Mail as PDF in Mail 196

Chapter 16: Contacts 198

Adding a Contact to Your Device 198

Updating an Existing Contact 198

Finding an Existing Contact 199

Sharing a Contact 200

Assigning Photos to Contacts 201

Deleting a Contact 202

Chapter 17: Calendar 203

Changing the Default Time Zone for Calendar Alerts 203

Selecting an Alternate Calendar 204

Managing Calendar Syncing 205

Setting Default Alert Times 205

Setting a Reminder to Leave on Time 206

Setting the start of Your Week 206

Setting a Default Calendar 207

How to turn events in Apps on and off 207

Creating a Calendar Event 208

Editing a Calendar Event 209

Deleting a Calendar Event 210

Moving a Calendar Event or Appointment by Dragging and Dropping 211

Sharing an Event 211

Creating a Calendar Event with Siri 212

Using Siri to Update a Calendar Event 213

Using Siri to View and Check Your Calendar 214

Using Siri to Cancel a Calendar Event 215

Chapter 18: Maps 216

Viewing and Sharing Your Current Location 216

Marking Your Current Location 216

Sharing Your Current Location 217

Changing Your Map View 217

Browsing or Searching a Location..........218

Finding Nearby Locations..........219

Selecting a Route in Maps..........220

Viewing Recent Map Searches..........222

Adding Favorite Locations in Maps..........222

Viewing Favorite Places in Maps..........223

Deleting Favorites from Maps..........223

Sharing Directions with Maps..........224

Getting Directions with Siri and Maps..........225

Using Siri and Maps to Locate Local Businesses..........226

Finding Your Way Home via Siri and Maps..........227

Changing the Navigation Voice Volume..........228

Deleting Recent Destination and Search History..........229

Viewing the Weather in Maps..........229

Opening Apple Maps Locations in Google Maps..........230

Chapter 19: Podcasts..........232

Finding, subscribing to and Streaming/downloading Podcasts..........232

Sharing Podcasts and Podcast Episodes..........233

Syncing Podcasts Across Devices..........233

Setting the Refresh Rate for Podcasts..........234

Turning off Delete Played Episodes for Podcasts..........234

Turning off Notifications for Podcasts..........235

Chapter 20: Find My..........236

Finding Friends in Find My..........236

Sharing your Location..........237

Notifying Friends of Your Location..........238

Marking a Device as Lost 240

Erasing a Device Remotely 241

Managing Your Personal Settings in Find My 243

Chapter 21: Face Time 245

Making a Face Time Audio or Video Call 245

Making a Group Facetime Call 245

Starting a Group FaceTime Call from a Group Messages Conversation 246

Adding a new Person to an existing Call 246

Switching from a Normal Call to Face Time 247

Turning off Video from a Face Time Call 247

Using Siri to Place a Face Time Call 248

Using Face Time with Apple TV 248

Introduction

The iPhone 12 min is new for 2020. It was launched by Apple on october 13th. The 5.4-inch iPhone 12 mini is geared towards users who can't step up to the higher end versions. Those who buy the mini won't miss out on so much tech and features because the mini packs a punch. Let's look at the specs: For a base price of $699, you get features like edge to edge super retina XDR display, a new ceramic shield front cover, the A14 bionic chip which is said to be the fastest ever in a smart phone, an advanced dual camera system, iOS 14 operating system with all its new and advanced features such as widgets, Apps library, App clips etc

The mini also has the new Magsafe high powered wireless charging system and an all new ecosystem of accessories that work seamlessly with the iPhone mini.

The mini is 5G capable and offers the broadest 5G coverage worldwide. It even features the smart data mode that extends battery life by measuring 5G needs and tries to balance data usage, speed and power. The mini has a water resistance rating of up to 6 meters for 30 minutes. The storage options are still the same. Users can choose from 64gb, 128gb and 256gb.

The colors are blue, red, green, black and white. The iPhone 12 mini however doesn't come with a power adapter and ear pods as part of Apple's drive to reduce carbon emissions and enable smaller and lighter packaging.

Now that we are done with the preliminaries, let's get to down to helping you navigate your way around your new device

Chapter 1: Setting up your new iPhone 12 mini

When you turn on your new iPhone for the first time, you'll be greeted with "Hello" in a variety of languages. It's basically the same even if you're starting from ground up, restoring from another iPhone, or switching from Android.

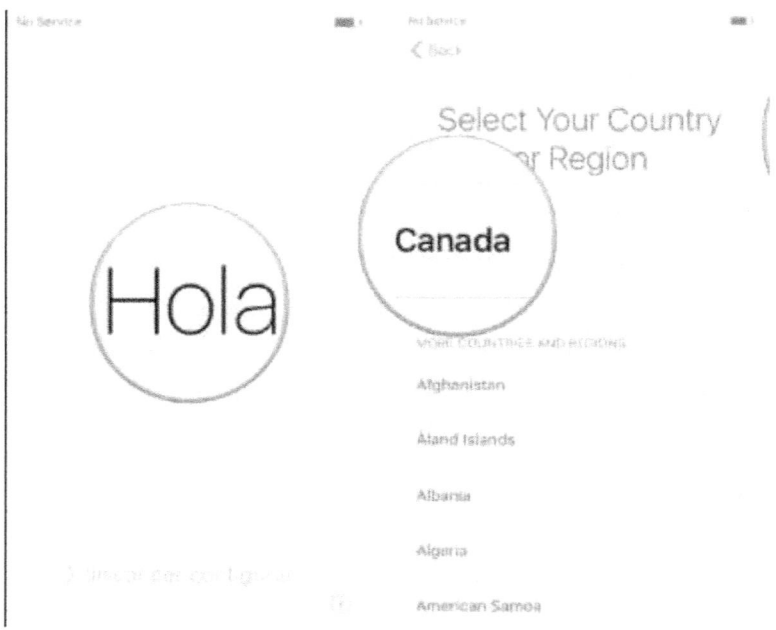

Moving Data and Stuff from A Previous Phone

Basically, you have three options to move data and settings from your old iPhone to a new iPhone. First, you can use the Quick Start feature which is the easiest one, restore from iTunes/Finder, and restore from iCloud. Just make sure you have backed up data of your old iPhone to iCloud or iTunes/Finder, just in case the Quick Start method fails. Be sure not to forget to update the software before you begin. For you to be able to use Quick Start, both devices have to run iOS 12 or later. Find below, the steps to set up iPhone 12 mini using the Quick Start option:

- The first step is to make sure both iPhones are plugged to power sources and Wi-Fi.
- Next you turn on your brand-new iPhone 12 mini and place it next to your previous iPhone.
- Once the Quick Start prompt appears on the old iPhone, click on **Continue**.
- Next, verify on your new iPhone 12 mini if there is an animation coming on its display. If it's there, then place your old iPhone on the top of the new one to scan the animation.

- Next, you put in your passcode on the new iPhone, the one that you use to unlock your previous iPhone.
- Now, on your new device, follow the on-screen instruction to set up the Face ID.
- When you get to the **Transfer Your Data** screen, tap **Transfer from iPhone** and let the process finish.

In case you don't have your old iPhone anymore, it's still possible for you to restore its contents to your new iPhone without stress. All you need do is follow the steps to set up iPhone 12 mini from iCloud or iTunes/Finder back up.

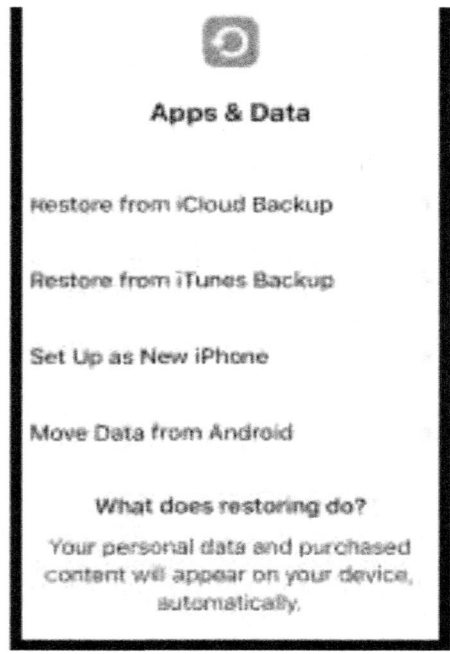

- Power on your new iPhone 12 mini by pressing and holding the power button on the top right of the phone until the Apple logo appears.

- Next, On the Quick Start screen, tap **Set Up Manually**.
- Next, select a Wi-Fi network and enter its password.
- Next, on the **Data & Privacy** screen, tap **Continue** after you read the statement.
- When you get to the next screen, tap **Continue** to set up Face ID.
- Now, create a 6-digit passcode or tap **Passcode Options** at the bottom of the screen to choose the other password type options. Re-enter the passcode you choose on the next screen to confirm.
- Next, On the **Apps & Data** screen, select **Restore from iCloud Backup** or **Restore from iTunes Backup**.
- Enter the Apple ID of your previous iPhone and the password.
- Click **Agree** to confirm that you have read the Terms and Conditions.
- Click the latest backup on the screen and tap **Continue** on the following screen.
- The restoring process may take several minutes to complete.

How to Set Up iPhone 12 mini As A New Phone
You can set up iPhone 12 mini as a new phone. The basic requirements before starting the setup process are an Apple ID and its password and an Internet connection.

- Power on the phone by pressing and holding the power button on the top right of your iPhone 12 mini and you will be greeted with a 'Hello' screen.
- Press the home button to continue the setup process.

- Select a language, then choose your country or region.
- On the Quick Start screen, select **Set up Manually**.
- Choose a WIFI network and enter the password. In case you have inserted a SIM card to your iPhone and have an active cellular data, select **Use Cellular Connection** at the bottom of the screen and select **Continue**.
- Next, follow the on-screen prompts to set up Face ID.
- when you are done setting up Face ID, choose **Set Up as New iPhone** on the **Apps & Data** screen. (more on the Face ID in a separate chapter)
- Now, enter your Apple ID and its password or select **Don't have an Apple ID or forgot it?** on the bottom of the screen. Next, follow the prompts to create a new Apple ID.
- When you get to the **Express Settings** screen, tap **Continue** or **Customize Settings**.
- Tap **Get Started** to start using your iPhone 12 mini.
- You have the option to customize the settings and add some apps later on.

Moving Data from an Android Device

If you have been using an android device and made the decision to join the apple family, you will need to transfer all your stuff from the android phone to your new iPhone 12 mini. The good news is that Apple has an app designed for new users making the switch from android to iOS. You can find it in the google play store. The first thing you need to do is to get the move to iOS on your android device. Note that you won't be able to transfer your android apps because they are not compatible with the Apple platform. You also won't be able to get your music and passwords moved too. Also keep in the mind that you can only transfer from an android device to an iPhone running iOS 9 or higher. All that being said, follow the guide below:

Set up your iPhone 12 mini till you get to the display titled: **"Apps & Data**

Click on the **"move Data from Android"** option

- From your android device, access the **google play store** and search for **"move to iOS"**
- Next, open the **move to iOS** listing.
- Click **install.**
- **Agree** to the permissions request

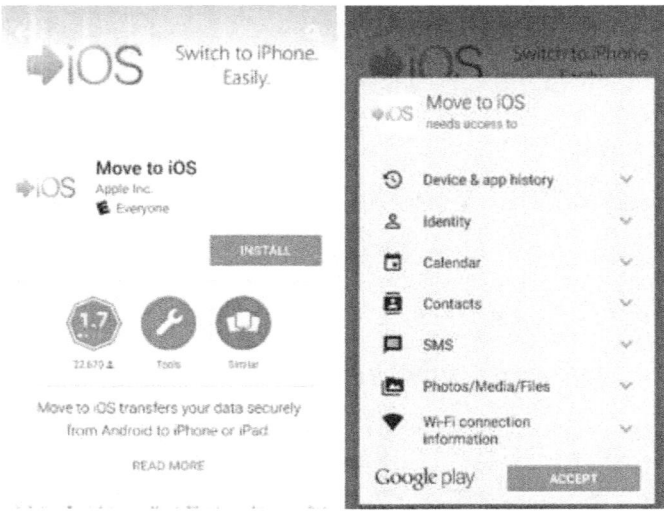

- **Open** after its installed.
- Click **continue** on both devices.

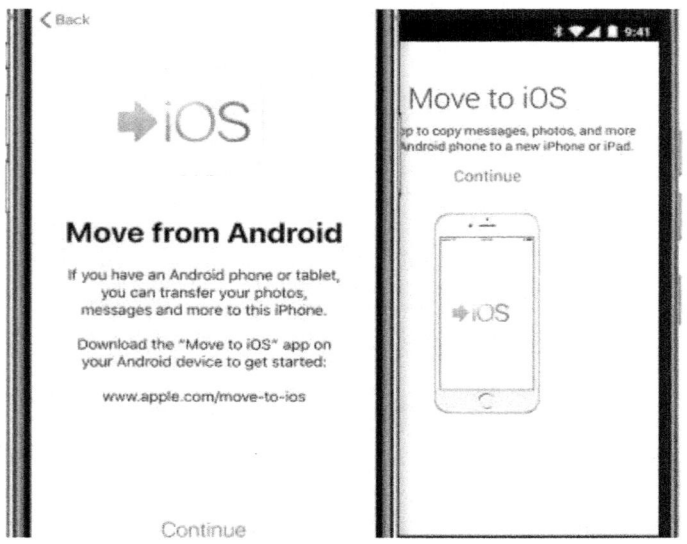

- Click **Agree** and then **Next** on your Android device
- From your **Android device**, key in the **12-digit** code shown on your iPhone 12 mini.

- When you key in the code, the two devices will connect over a wi-fi connection and identify the data that can be moved in between both of them.
- You will be asked if you would like to move your google account information, chrome book marks, contacts, messages, photos and videos etc.
- Your android device will move the selected data to your new iPhone Once the data transfer is done, select continue setting up your iPhone and set up a new Apple ID or if you happen to already have an existing one, you can log in.

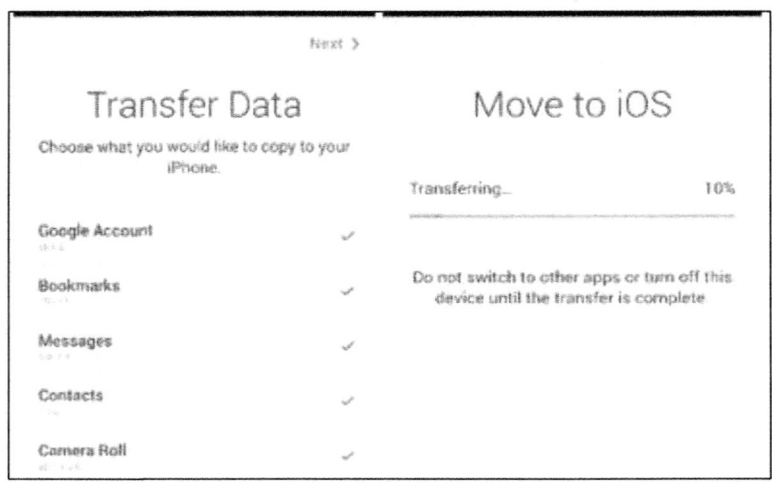

When you have completed the set-up process, you will be asked to log in to the accounts you just moved from your old Android device and that's it. You can begin to use your new device.

Moving Data To Your iPhone VIA iCloud
If you are inclined towards this option, then find below, the process you Can utilize to get it done:

- Go to **Settings** on your old device as shown above.
- Select the **Apple ID** banner
- Select **iCloud**

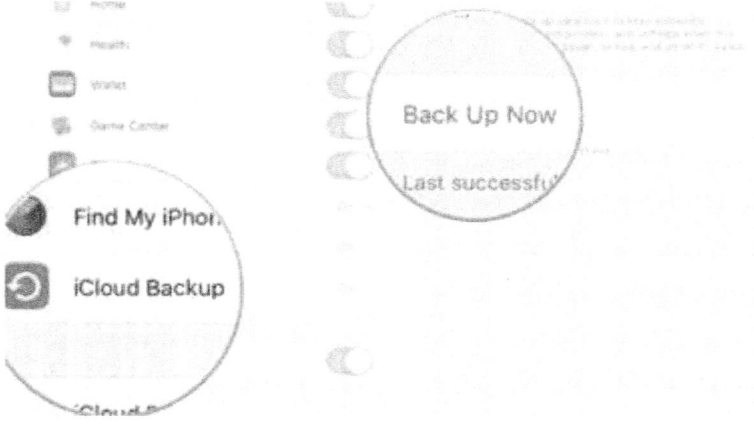

23

- Select **Back up now.**
- Power off your old device when the backup is done and take out the **sim card** from the old device especially if you are going to use it in the new iPhone.
- The backup must be completed before you move ahead to the next step.
- Next, you place the **sim** into the new device; that's if you want to use it in the new phone and power on the backed up new device.
- Push the home button and obey the prompts to select your preferred language and activate your wi-fi network.
- Next, you sign in to your **iCloud account**.
- Select **next** and then select **Agree**
- Repeat the above step (select agree) and Select the **backup** just completed.

You are done. Move on with setting up your new iPhone 12 mini.

Transferring Your Data via the macOS Catalina Option
- Tether your old iPhone to your Mac computer which should be running macOS Catalina.

- Next, tap on the **finder** icon in the bar to get directed to a fresh finder window.
- Tap on your **iPhone** under the **locations** display
- You will next be asked to **trust** your iPhone.
- Next, you will click the **checkbox** for **Encrypt local Backup.**
- You will be required to Setup a **password** If this your first use of encrypted backups.
- Select **Backup now.**
- When you are done, disconnect your **old iPhone** and shut it down. If you intend to use the **sim** in your old device in the new one, take it out.
- When the backup is done, transfer the **sim** to the new **iPhone** and power it up.
- Once again, tether the **new iPhone** to the Mac.
- Push the home button on your **iPhone** and obey the set-up prompts.
- Next, click **Restore from Mac or PC** and Select your new iPhone from **locations** in the finder window and tap **Restore from this backup as shown:**

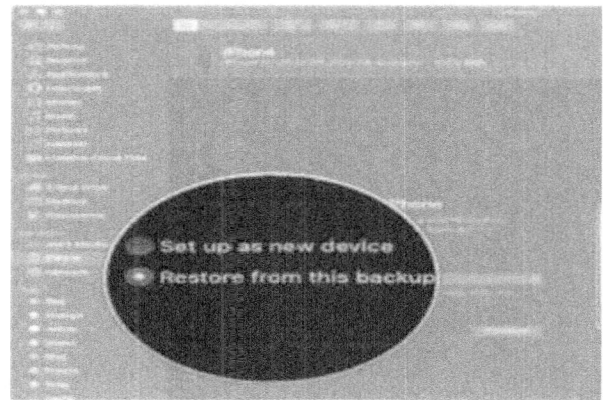

- Select your **recent backup** from the drop-down options and select **Continue.**

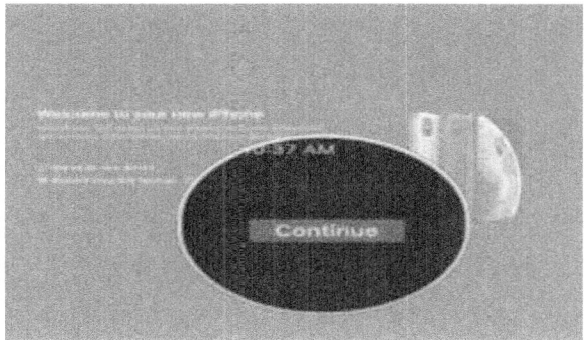

- Key in your **password** and tap **Restore** if you did an encrypted backup if you are interrogated by the finder.

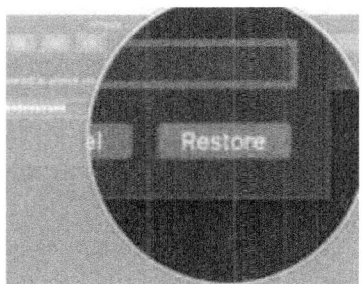

That's it. You all done. You can now move on with the remaining part of setting up your new iPhone 12 mini.

Moving your data via macOS Mojave and older

- You have to have the latest version of **iTunes.**
- Connect your **old iPhone** to your **mac system.**
- Open **iTunes.**
- Tap on the iPhone icon in the **menu** bar

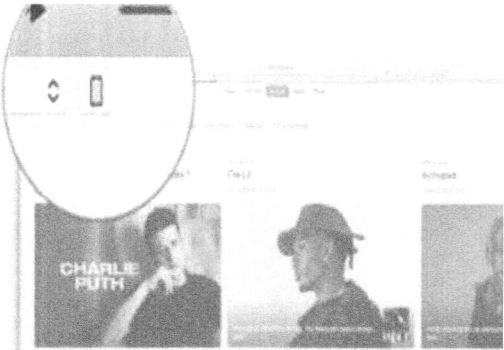

- Select **Encrypt backup.** You may be required to set-up a **password** if it's your first time encrypting a backup.

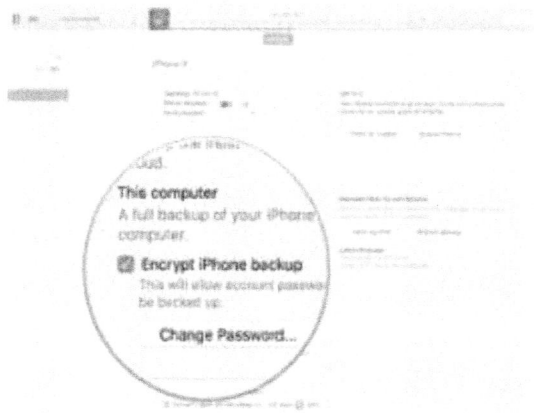

- Next, select **Backup now.**

- Disregard **Backup apps** if it comes up.
- Disconnect your **old device** when the **backup** process is complete.
- Remove your **sim** from the **old iPhone** if you plan to reuse it in the **new iPhone** and then wait for the **backup** process to run.
- When you are ready to resume, equip the new iPhone with the sim (either previous used or new sim).
- Switch on the new device and connect it to your Mac. Obey the set-up directions till you activate your wi-fi.
- Click **Restore from iTunes** backup.
- From your Mac or windows PC, opt for **Restore from this backup.**
- Select the most **recent backup** from the options.

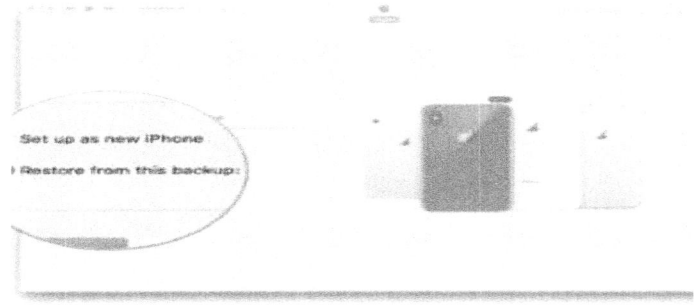

28

- Select **Continue**.
- Finally, in case you are prompted, key in your **password** if the backup was encrypted.

At this point, you have to keep your new device connected to iTunes till the transfer is executed which in some cases, may take a little bit of time based on the amount of data being moved.

Chapter 2: The Face ID

The Face ID is a biometric authentication security feature designed by Apple that uses a camera to scan a user's face and gather details. With it, users can not only unlock their device but they can also authorize Apple pay payments, confirm iTunes and app store purchases among other uses. So, let's look at the steps to set-up this feature.

Setting up the Face ID on the iphone 12 mini

To set up the Face ID function, you would have begun the process of the initial set-up of a new or restored iPhone and gotten to the point where you would be asked to choose either to set-up the Face ID immediately or later. So, either way or option, the process runs as below:

- Open the **Settings** app from the home screen display.
- Click on **Face ID & Passcode**
- Enter your passcode for authentication if interrogated. You would be required to set one up if you didn't do so when you were setting up your new device.

- Tap **Set Up Face ID**. Tap **Get Started**
- Do your first **scan** by slowly moving your head in a circle

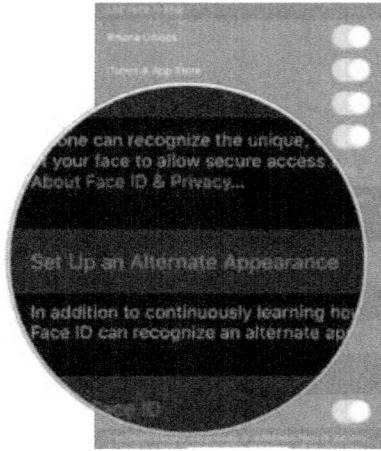
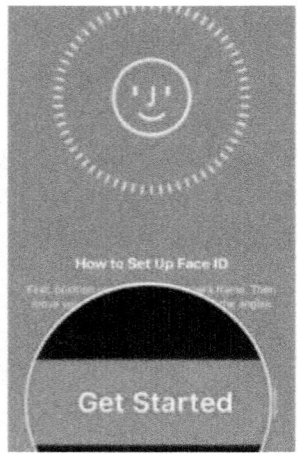

- Tap **Continue**
- Repeat the **scan** a second time and then tap **Done**

Turning Off Require Attention for Face ID

You have to look directly at your face ID enabled phone before it would recognize you and unlock. If you want to unlock without looking directly at the screen, follow the directions below:

- Go to **settings**. Tap **Face ID & Passcode**. Enter your **Passcode**
- Switch the **Require Attention for Face ID** button to off. The system still has to see your eyes, nose and mouth
- Tap **Ok.** you can switch Require Attention back on when you want

Resetting Face ID

In case you want to switch the face registered on your device or for any other reason, do the following:

- Go to **settings**. Tap **Face ID & Passcode**. Enter your **Passcode**
- Tap **Reset Face ID**

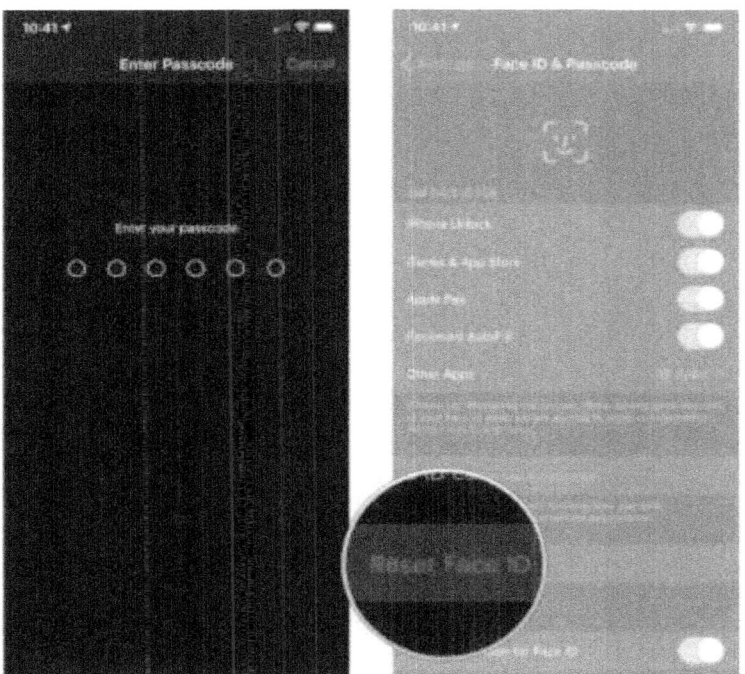

Adding a second Face to Face ID
- Go to settings.
- Tap Face ID & Passcode.
- Enter Passcode.
- Tap **Set up an Alternate Appearance**
- Follow the instructions on the screen to finish the set up for the other user. You can only store one primary face ID and one alternate. In case you want to change the secondary one, you will have to reset Face ID

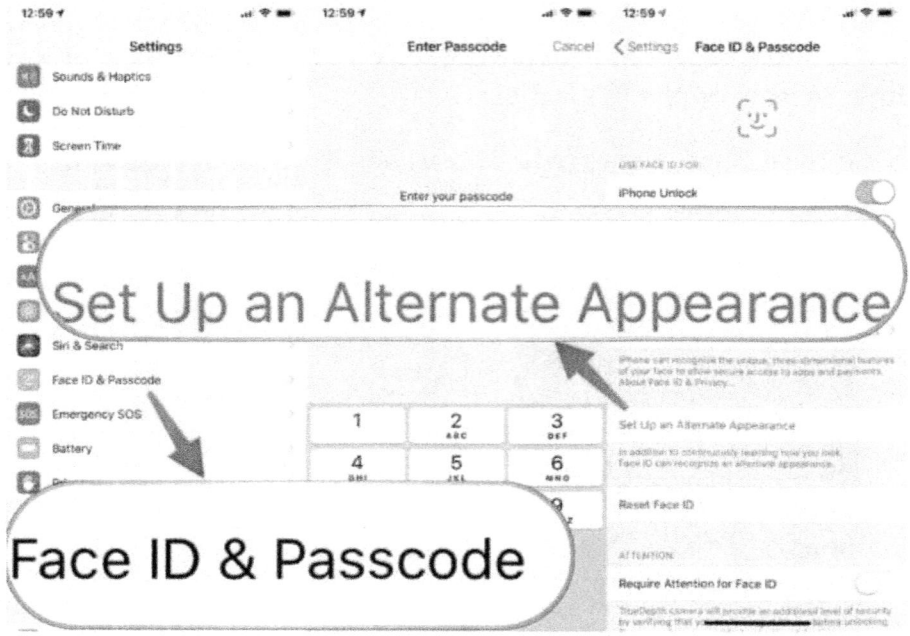

Using Face ID to Unlock, Apple Pay, App Store Purchases etc
- Go to settings. Tap Face ID & Passcode. Enter Passcode.
- Next, turn the switches for **iPhone unlock, Apple Pay, iTunes & App store, Safari AutoFill on or off** based on your preference

Managing Face ID Use with Apps

For apps that support biometric authorization, you can manage them in settings and turn them on or off

- Go to **settings**. Tap **Face ID & Passcode**. Enter your **Passcode**
- Tap **other Apps**
- Turn **switches** for the apps that have requested to use Face ID on or off

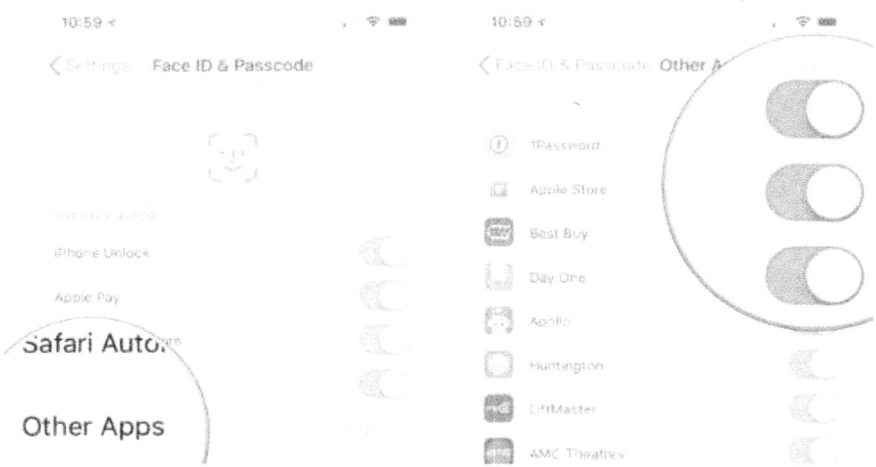

Managing Attention Features for Face ID
- Go to **settings**.
- Tap **Face ID & Passcode.**
- Enter **Passcode**
- Turn the switch next to **Require Attention for Face ID** on or off
- Turn the switch next to **Attention Aware Features** on or off

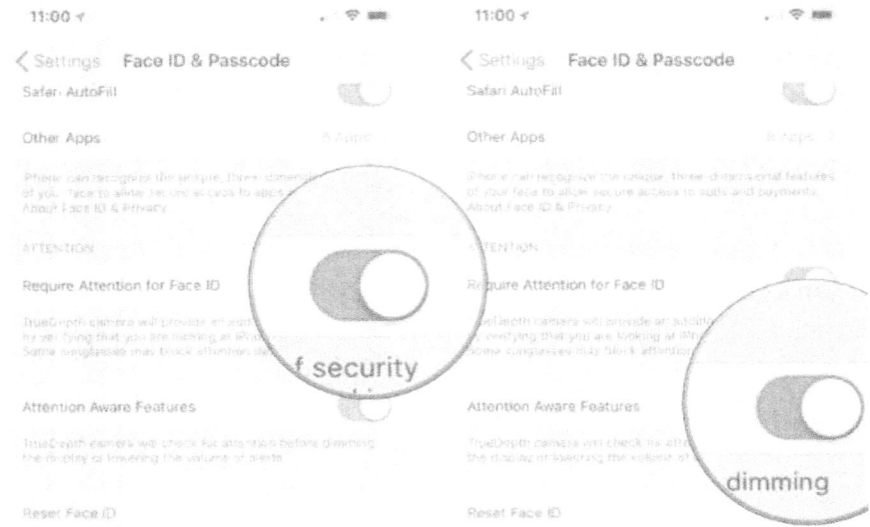

Disabling Face ID Temporarily
- Push and hold the wake and one of the volume buttons at the same time
- Tap **Cancel** or the side button if you want to unlock your phone
- Key in your **password** when next you want to unlock the device. Face ID should work normally

Chapter 3: Setting up "Hey Siri"

During the initial setting up process of your new device, you will be asked if you would ike to use the "Hey Siri" voice activation option. If you elect to activate it later, find below, the process of doing so:

- Open **Settings** from your home screen
- Click on **Siri & Search**
- Select the **"listen for 'Hey siri"** button to turn it on.

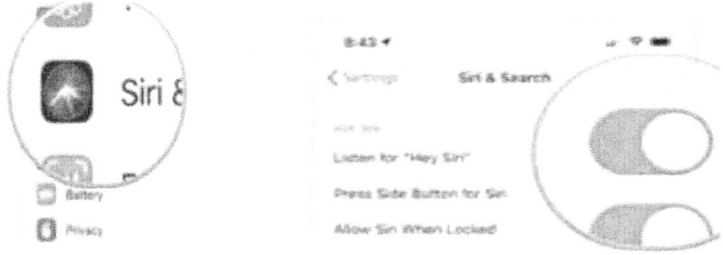

You will need to train the technology to recognize your voice.

- Click on **continue** on the set up **"Hey Siri"** page
- Next, say **"Hey Siri"** using your voice
- Say again **"Hey siri send a message"**

36

- To get further used to the technology and for the virtual assistant to register your voice, from the screen display, you will be prompted to make some statements like:

'"hey siri, How's the weather today?"

"hey siri, set a timer for three minutes"

"Hey siri, play some music"

- Finally, click **done** on the "Hey siri" is ready display.

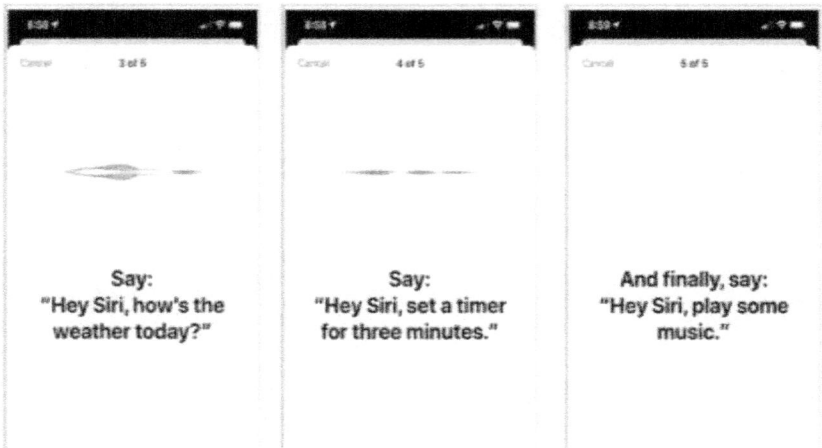

If you get it done properly, then siri would have registered your voice and is now at your service.

Using "Hey siri"

- Make sure you are situated within proper audio range of your device.
- Next, speak loudly for your device to pick up:" **Hey siri"**
- Let **"Hey siri"** know the task you want it to carry out. For e.g., set an alarm for 5am, call Jason on speaker, etc.

Chapter 4: Setting up Apple ID

The Apple ID is an Apple account that allows you to purchase stuff or items from the apple store like books, movies, Apps, games, movies, and music from iTunes, sync your contacts, reminders, and calendars through iCloud and use iMessage and Facetime in the messages apps. If you already have an apple ID, then you only need sign in with your apple ID but if this is your first apple device, you need to create one. Find how to go about it below:

Creating an Apple ID

- Go to the **Settings** app.
- On the top of the screen, click on **Sign in to your iPhone**.

- Tap on **Don't have an Apple ID or forgot it?**
- On the following screen, choose **Create Apple ID**

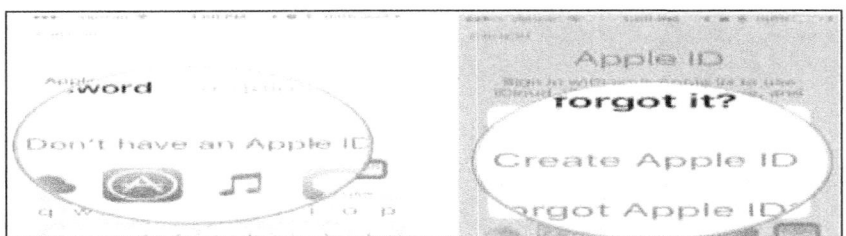

- Next, key in your date of birth and click on **Next**.
- Enter your name: first and last and click on **Next**.

- Select to **sign up with a current email address** or if you would prefer to **get a free iCloud email address**.

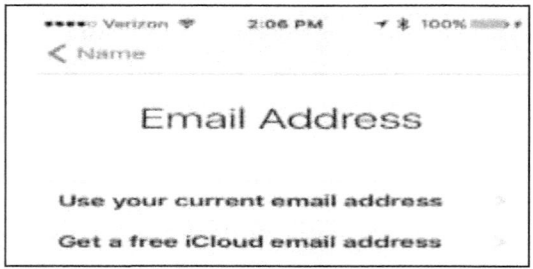

- enter your email address and create your chosen **password**.
- Repeat the **password**.
- Next, you are to select three security questions and enter the answers to the chosen questions and click on next.

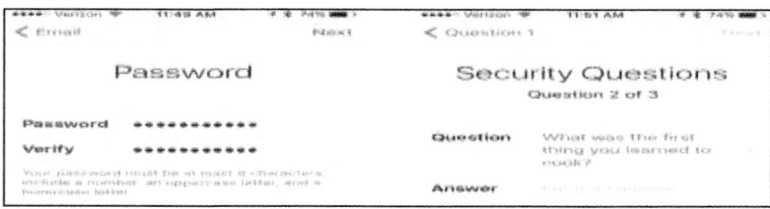

- Next, **Agree** to the Terms and Conditions.
- You can decide to Merge or not to merge, to sync iCloud data from calendars, contacts, Safari, and reminders.

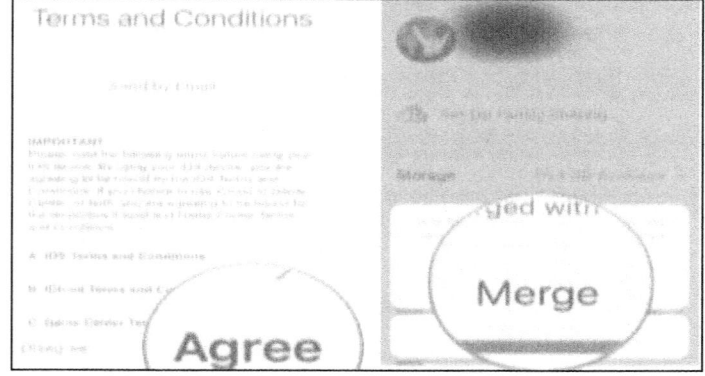

39

- Select **Ok** to agree that you want the **Find My** enabled.

Signing In to iCloud With an Existing Apple ID
- Go to the **Settings** app.
- Next, on top of the screen, click on **Sign in to your iPhone.**
- Enter your login details and click **Sign In.**

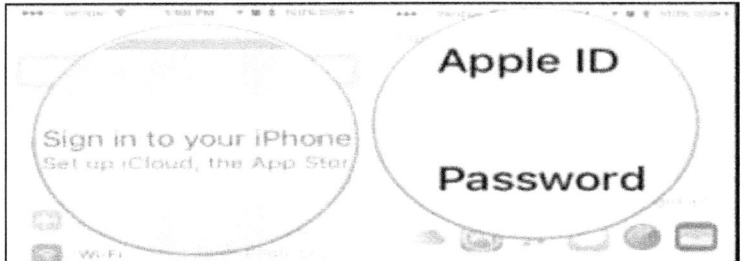

- Enter your **password** when required

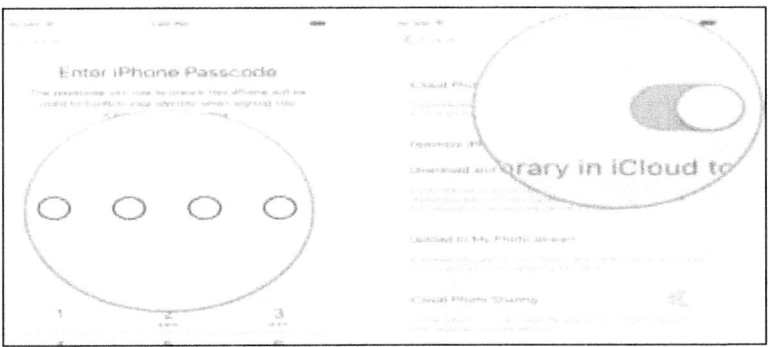

- Activate or deactivate the option for Apps using iCloud, based on your preferred settings.

Signing Out of iCloud
- From the **Settings** app, go to the top of the screen and select your **Apple ID**.
- Scroll to the bottom of the screen and click on **Sign Out.**

- Enter your Apple ID password for this account and select **Turn Off.**
- Turn on the buttons for all the data you want to retain on your iPhone.
- From the top right side of the screen, click **Sign Out.**
- Click again on **Sign Out** to affirm what you have just done.

Chapter 5: Setting up Apple Pay

With Apple pay, it's possible for users to purchase items either online or in-store. All it would entail is just a touch of the Home button and a scan of your fingerprint; But before you can start using it, you have to set it up first. Here's how:

The first step is to add a card to Apple pay.

- Open the **Wallet** app from the home screen display.

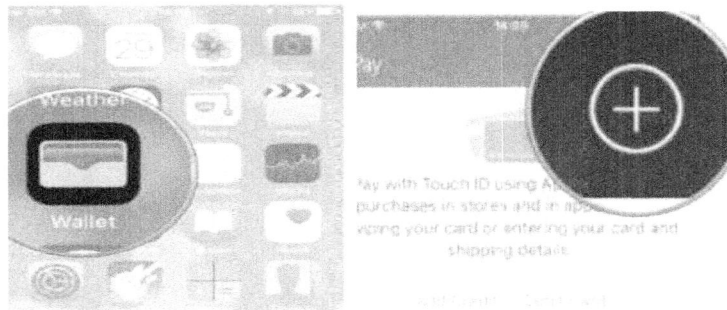

- Click on the **+button** on the top right side of the screen
- Click on **Continue** or **Next** on the Apple pay screen

- Next, you have 2 options for entering the details of your credit or debit card. Either you **manually** input them or you **scan with the**

phone camera. (should you decide to go with the camera scan option, make sure that the credit or debit card has embossed numbers because, the photo detection system does not register flat numbers)

- Click **Next** on the card details display screen.
- Input the **expiration date** and **security code** of the card manually.

- Click **Next**
- Click **Agree** to accept the terms and conditions
- Click **Agree** again.

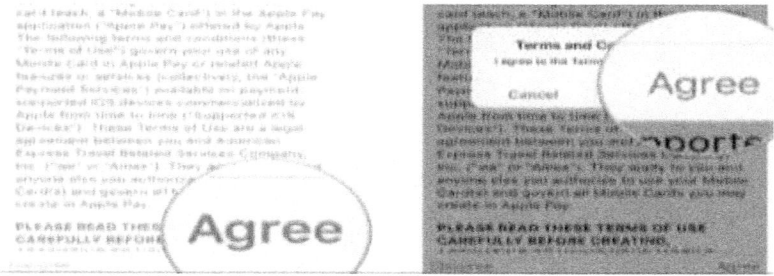

- Select **Next** after you choose verification method and tap **Enter code.**
- Key in the verification code that was given you. This could either be a text, call or email based on your chosen verification method.

43

 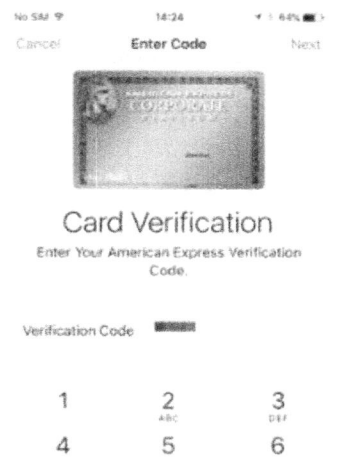

- Click on **Next** and then click on **Done**.

Follow this same procedure in case you ever wish to add more debit or credit cards.

Changing the Initial Card for Apple Pay
The apple pay system allows you to register and effect payment for purchases and transactions using several credit and debit cards. You can seamlessly switch between them to make payments.

- Go to the **Settings** app on your device
- Open **Wallet & Apple pay**

- Click on **Default card**

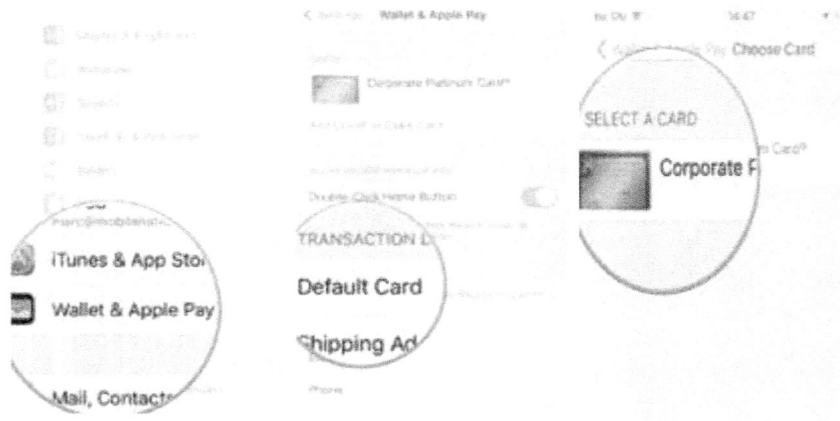

- Select the card you would prefer to use as the standard for making purchases and transactions.

Removing a Card from Apple Pay
- Go to **Settings**
- Click on **wallet & Apple pay**

- Click on the **card** you would like to remove
- Finally, click on **Remove this card**

45

Chapter 6: Setting up and using the haptic touch

The haptic touch is a new way to perform and get your device to carry out tasks. It simply involves long pressing to activate actions. It lets you do more effortlessly.

Rearranging or deleting Apps on the Home screen with Haptic touch

- Long press on the Home screen icon you want to open quick for

- Now click on task you want to execute

Widgets

- For widgets, long press on the home screen icon you want to call up widgets for.

- Click on the **widget** to go to access the tap.

In case you are downloading apps, there are steps you can take to give priority to one specific App over the others and canceling the ones you no longer need.

- **Long press** on the installation icon you want to open quick actions

 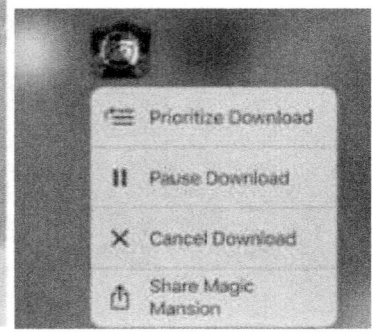

- Next, click on the action you want to perform
- Click on the action you want to execute

Using Haptic Touch with Notifications
- Long press on a **Notification**

- Click on the **notification** and click on the **X button** to dismiss the notification

With Haptic touch, you can wipe the notification center

- Long press on the **x button** above your notifications

- Click on **clear all notifications**

Customizing the Haptic Touch
- Open **Settings** from your home screen

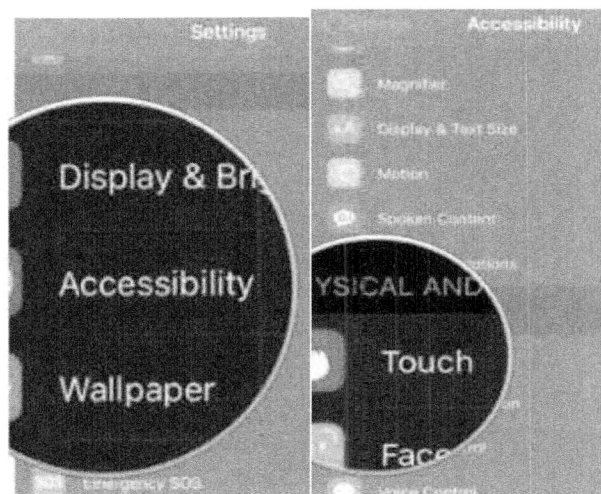

- Click on **Accessibility**

48

- Click on **Touch**
- Click on **Haptic touch** and select either **fast** or **slow** to change the time it takes to set off the Haptic touch.

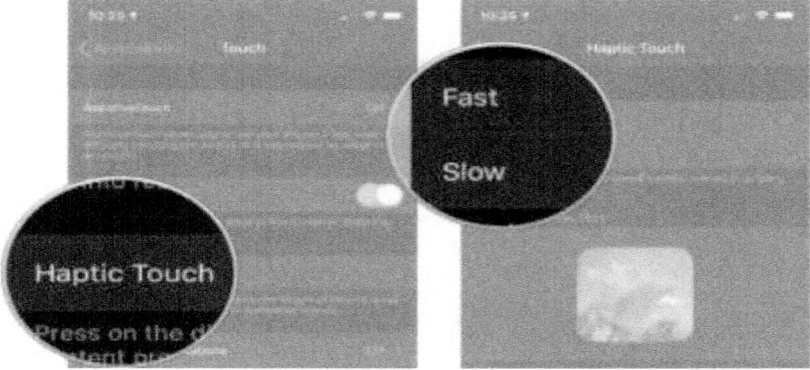

Chapter 7: iOS 14 features and functions

iOS 14 is the latest operating system from Apple. It has new features and functions meant to make the iphone more up to date and afford users access to do a whole lot more.

Moving Widgets to the Home Screen from Today View

- Open **Today view** by Swiping from left edge of the **Home Screen**
- Navigate or scroll to find the widget
- **Tap and hold** till t starts jiggling and drag it off the right side of the screen
- Next, place it where you want it to be by dragging it on the **Home Screen**

Adding a Widget to a Home Screen Page

- On the **Home Screen page** where you want to place the widget, tap and hold the **Home Screen background** till all apps starts jiggling

- Next, tap the cross at the screen top to launch the widgets gallery
- Locate the widget you want, **tap it and swipe left** to view the size options
- After you see a preferred widget, tap **Add Widget** and tap **Done**

Editing a Widget
- **Tap and hold a Widget** on your home screen to launch a quick actions menu
- Next, **tap Edit Widget** and select options
- Incase it's a smart stack, **tap Edit Stack**
- Tap **Home Screen**

Removing a widget from the Home Screen
- **Tap and hold the widget** to launch the quick actions menu
- Next, tap **Remove Widget** or **Remove Stack** as the case maybe

Viewing the Today View from your Lock screen
- Launch **Settings.** Tap **FaceID & Passcode.** Key in the **passcode.**
- Switch on **Today View**

Using the App Library

- **Swipe left** past all Home Screen pages to locate the App Library
- **Tap an App** in the Library to launch it
- To expand a Category that has more Apps below the top level, tap **the small icons** to see all
- Use the **search field** at screen top to view an alphabetical list of apps. To find a particular app, type its name in the **search field**
- To use the quick actions menu, **touch and hold an app**

Adding new Apps from the App store to the Home screen and App Library or App Library Only

- Launch **Settings.** Tap **Home Screen.** Tap **Add to Home Screen** or **App Library Only**

Hiding and Showing Home Screen Pages

- From the Home Screen, **tap and hold any app.** Tap **Edit Home Screen**
- When the Apps start Jiggling, **tap the dots** at screen bottom and you would view thumbnail images of your Home screen pages
- **Tap to remove** the checkmarks under the thumbnails of the unwanted pages
- To re-add the hidden pages, **tap the checkmarks**
- **Tap Done** twice to finish

App Clips

Use an app clip to carry out quick tasks without having to download and install the complete app. App clips can be used in safari, Maps, Messages or for parking, renting a bike, ordering food etc

Getting and using an App Clip

- To open an app clip, tap the **app clip link** in Safari, Maps or Messages
  You could also use the **phone camera to scan the QR code** at the physical location

You could also use NFC (near-field communications) by holding your phone close to the tag
- The app clip card would show at screen bottom

- Use **Sign in with Apple** and make a payment **using Apple Pay** from supported app clips
- To locate a recently used app clip, launch the **App library** and tap **Recently Added**
- To remove app clips, launch **Settings.** Tap **App Clips.** Tap **Remove All Clips**

Using the Translate App
Use the app to translate voice and text for supported languages.

- **Rotate your iphone to portrait mode** while you are in the **translate tab** and **tap Translate**
- Choose the **language** from **screen top**

- Tap **Enter text. Type a sentence.** Tap **Go**. You could also dictate or say it out by tapping and saying the phrase

Translating a Conversation
This works in the split screen mode. If you have downloaded languages, it would work even without internet.

- **Rotate your phone to landscape mode** while in the Translate tab
- Tap the **microphone icon** and speak in any of the two languages

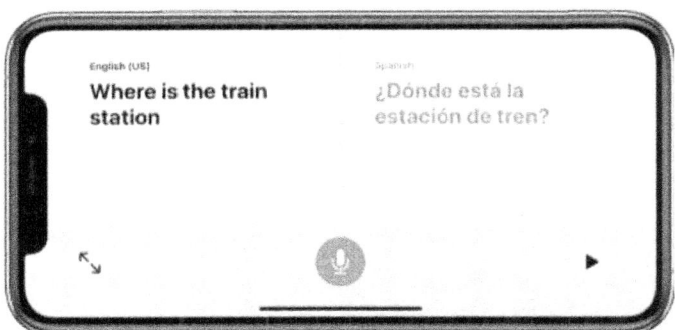

Downloading Languages for Offline Translation
- Tap the **Translate tab.** Tap **a language** at screen top
- Navigate down to **Available Offline Languages.** Tap the **selected languages** you want to download. Tap **Done**

Using the Search Function
You can use search on iPhone to find things like contacts, Mail and Messages, webpages etc

Selecting Apps Accessible in Search
- Launch **Settings.** Tap **Siri and Search.** Navigate down, choose **and tap** an App. **Turn Show in Search** on or off

How to search
- From the middle of your Home Screen**, swipe down**
- **Tap search field** and enter what you are looking for
- **Tap a suggested app** to launch it
- Tap **X in the search field** to start a new search

Searching in Apps
- In an app that has the search field or button, **tap the search field or tap the magnifying glass icon**
- If no search field is evident, **swipe down** from top
- Next, type your search and tap **Search**

Using the picture in picture function

This function allows you to carry out other tasks or use other apps while watching a video

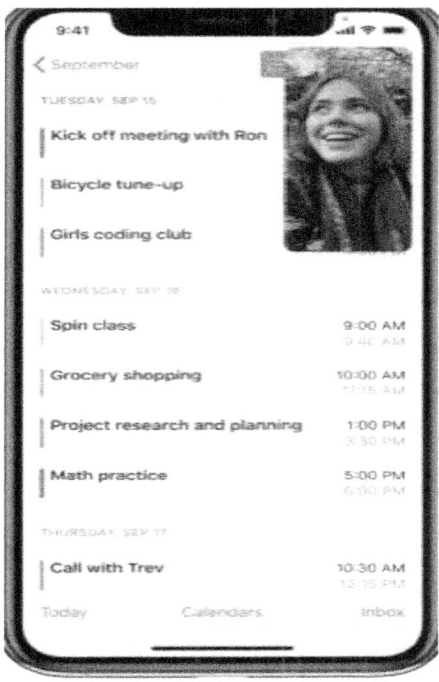

- As you are watching a video or using FaceTime, tap . This would reduce the video and move it to a screen corner so you can open and view other apps
- To increase the size of the video window, **pinch open.** To reduce it, **pinch closed**
- **Tap the video window** if you want to view the controls
- To move the video window, **drag it** to a new part of the screen

- If you want to hide the video window, **drag it** off the left or right edge of the screen
- Tap **X** anytime you want to close the window
- If you want to revert back to a full video screen, tap ⬚ again in the small video window

Messages: pinning a Conversation
Use this function to prioritize important messages

- To pin a conversation, **swipe right and tap the pin or tack icon**
- You could also **tap and hold a conversation** to drag it to top of the list
- To unpin a conversation, do any of the above actions in reverse

Switching from a Messages conversation to FaceTime or Audio Call
- From a Messages conversation, **tap the profile picture or name** at conversation top
- Next tap **FaceTime or audio**

Mentioning people in a conversation

Use this feature to call a contact's attention to a particular message.

- From a conversation, **start typing a contact's name** in the **name field**
- **Tap the name** when it shows

Replying to a Specific Message in a Conversation

- Open a conversation. **Double-tap or touch and hold** the specific message and tap
- Next, type your reply and tap

Designing your very own Memoji

- While in a Conversation, tap 🖼 and tap +
- Next **choose and tap each feature and options** you want to bring your character to life
- When you finish, tap **Done** and it would be added to your collection
- If at any time, you want to duplicate, edit or delete a Memoji, tap 🖼 and tap ⋯

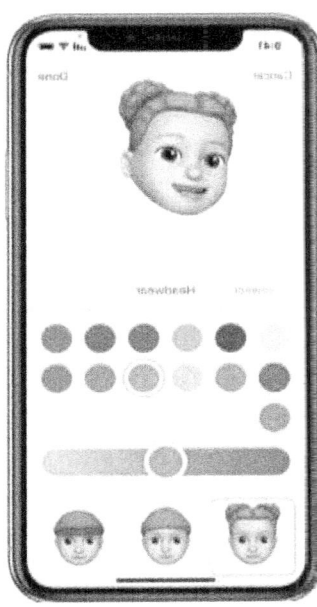

Using the Health App to set up Sleep Schedules

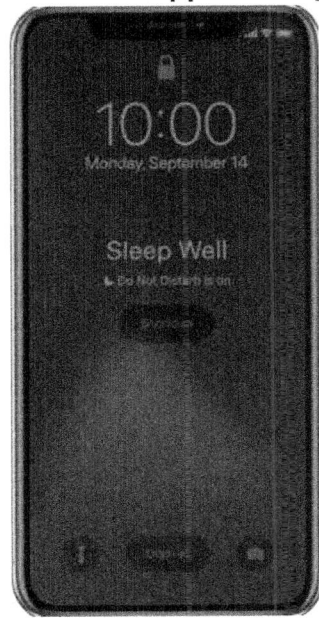

- To set up a sleep schedule, tap **Browse** at bottom right and tap **Sleep**

- Next, **swipe up** and tap **Get Started** just under **Set up Sleep**
- Follow the directions

Making Changes to your next Alarm
- From bottom right, tap **Browse** and tap **Sleep**
- Navigate down to your time table and tap **Edit**
- To make changes to your time table for going to bed and waking up, **drag** 🛏 **and** 🔔
- Next, select alarm options and tap **Done** when you finish

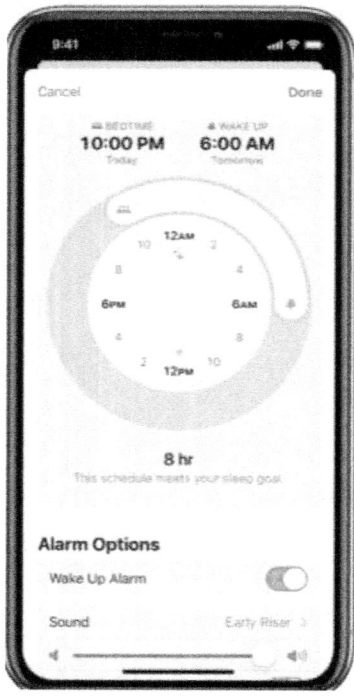

Changing or adding a sleep schedule
- From bottom right, tap **Browse** and tap **Sleep**
- Next, Navigate down to your Schedule. Tap full **schedule & options**
- Tap **Edit** to change a sleep schedule
- To add a sleep schedule, tap **Add Schedule for Other Days**

- If you want to switch off all sleep schedules, from bottom right, tap **Browse**, tap **Sleep,** tap **Full Schedule & Options.** Turn off **Sleep Schedule at screen top**

Changing your Wind Down Schedule and Activity

Wind down activities like reading or playing music appear on the lock screen if sleep mode is in effect

- From bottom right, tap **Browse**, tap **Sleep**, tap **Full Schedule & Options**
- To change when to activate sleep mode, **tap Wind Down** and choose a time
- Tap **Wind Down Short cuts** to add or remove an activity

Using the Health Checklist Function to Manage Health Features

- From top right, tap **your profile picture or initials**

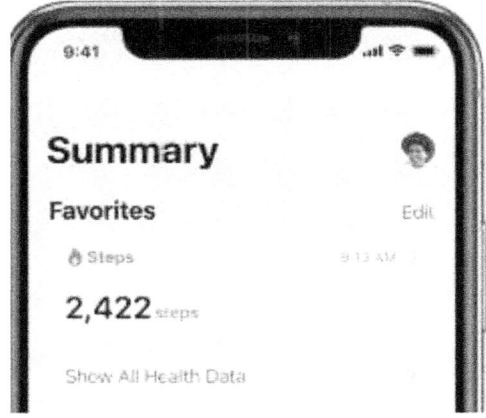

- Next, tap **Health Checklist**
- To activate or learn more about an item in the list, **tap on it**
- Tap **Back** to return to the checklist
- If your picture or initials are not in evidence, tap **Summary** or **Browse** at screen bottom and navigate back to screen top

62

Chapter 8: Setting Up and Using the Control Center

The control center gives the user easy and quick access on their device to quite a number of functions and features. It's possible for owners to execute actions right from the control center. Here's how:

- Open **Settings**
- Click on **Face ID & Passcode**
- Key in your **passcode** when required
- Navigate down and activate the **control center** button

How to Open the Control Center on Your Device
- From the bottom edge of the screen, swipe up towards the top of the screen

Customizing the Control Center

The control center allows the user the ability to choose the functions that can be accessed via the control center.

Adding Controls to the Control Center
The first step is to make sure that you have the control center feature or function enabled on your device.

- Go to the **Settings** App

63

- Click **control center**

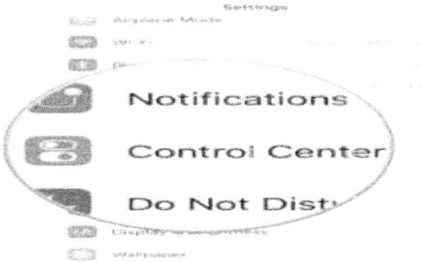

- Click on **Customize Controls**
- Click the **add button** (+) next to a control under the more controls display

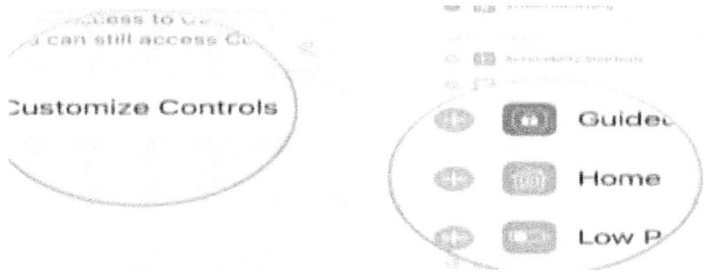

Organizing the Hierarchy of Controls in the Control Center

In case a user wants to organize the control center in such a way that the more frequently used functions are easily and readily accessed while the less used ones are placed at a lower position, here are the steps to follow:

- Go to the **Settings App** and click on **Control Center**
- Press and hold a **control** till it goes into hover mode
- Next, drag the **control** to its new place on the list

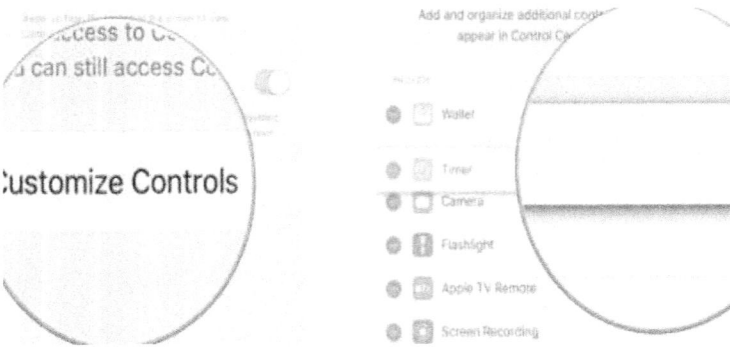

You can play around with the control center till it fits your desired setting and appearance.

Removing Controls from the Control Center
- Open the **settings App** and click **control center**
- Click **customize controls**
- Click the **remove button** which looks like this **(-)**. It's usually next to a control under the include section.

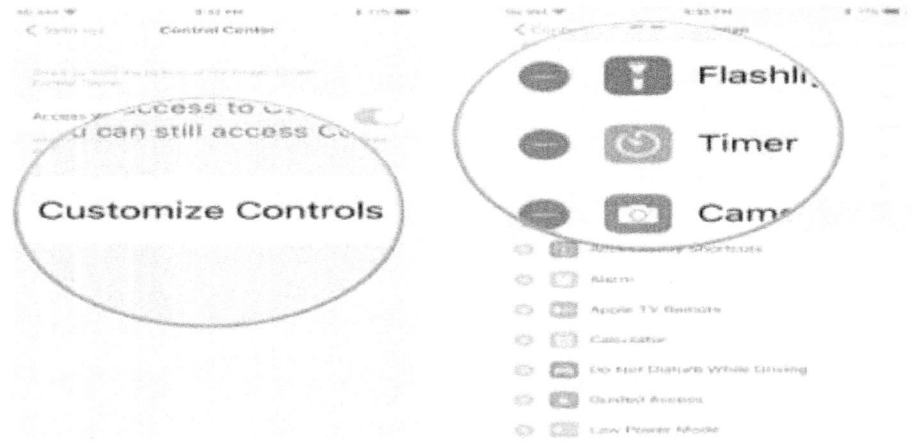

Disabling Control Center on the Lock Screen
- Open the **settings** App
- Click the **Face ID & Passcode**
- Key in your **Passcode**

- Navigate down and deactivate the **Control Center** button

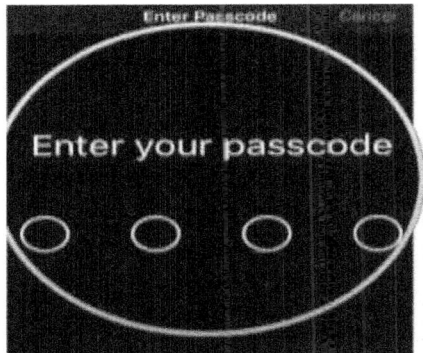
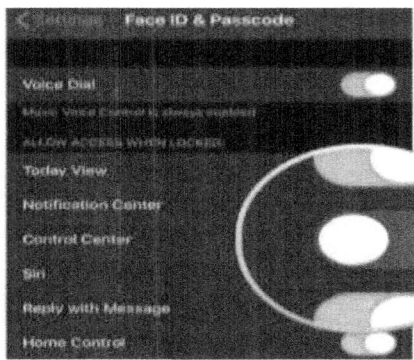

Disabling the Control Center from Apps
- Go to **Settings** and click **Control Center**
- Deactivate the **Access within Apps** button

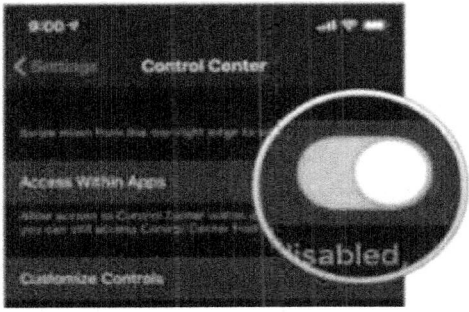

Chapter 9: Adjusting settings
Making Text Bolder and Bigger
- Open **Settings** and click **Accessibility**
- Click **Display and Text size**

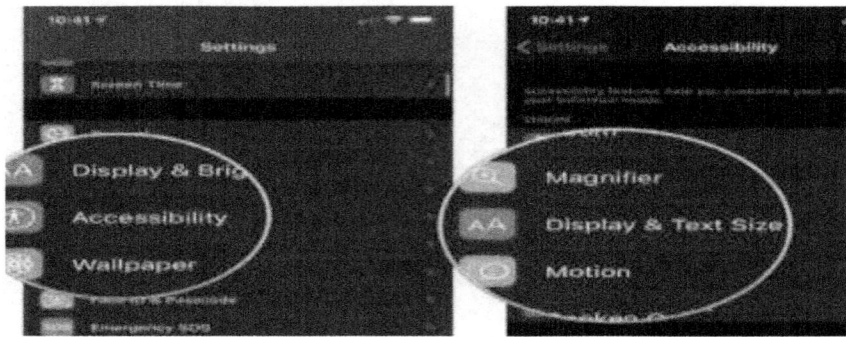

- Click **Larger Text**
- **Click,** hold and then drag the **slider** to change the text size
- In case you need the text to be even larger, click the button next to **Larger Accessibility Sizes**

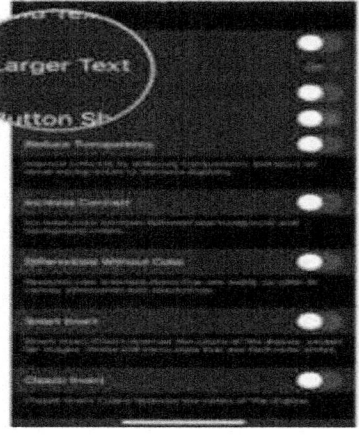
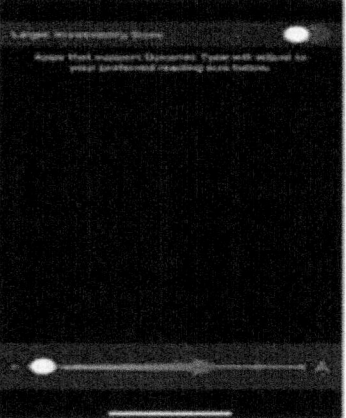

Changing the Text Buttons
- Open **Settings** and click **Accessibility**

- Click **Display and Text size**
- Next, tap the button next to **button shapes**

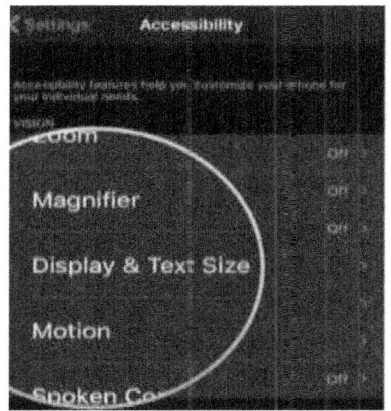
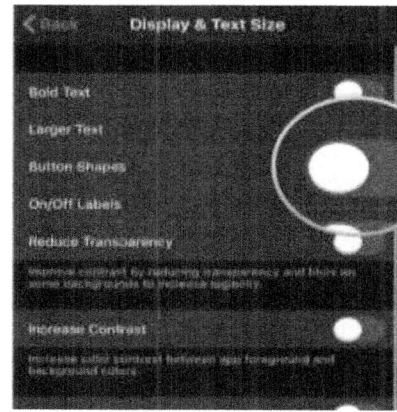

Reducing the White Point
- Launch **Settings** and **click Accessibility**
- Click **Display & Text size**
- Click the button next to **reduce white point**

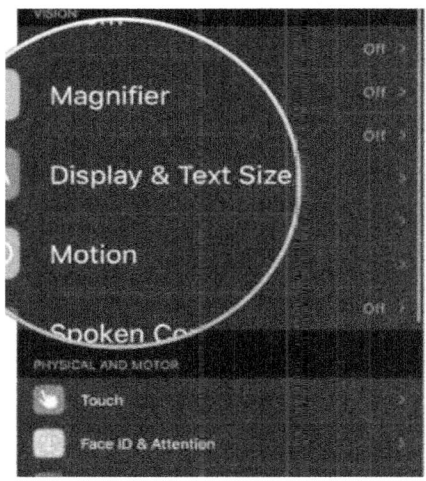
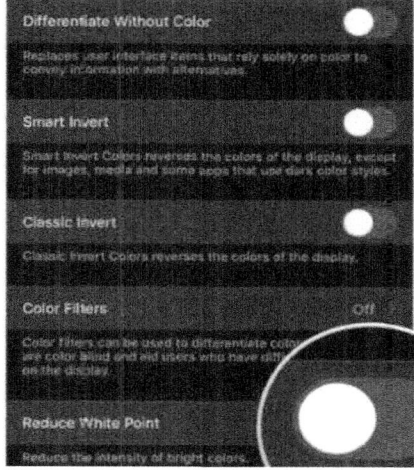

Deactivating Parallax and App Zooms
- Open **Settings** and click **Accessibility**
- Click **Motion**

68

- Activate the **button** next to **reduce motion** to the green "on" setting to activate **reduced motion**

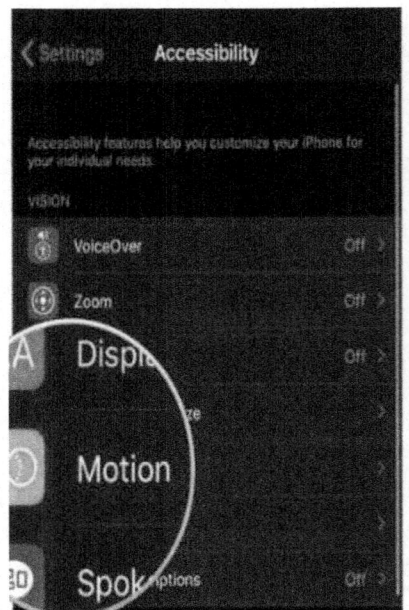 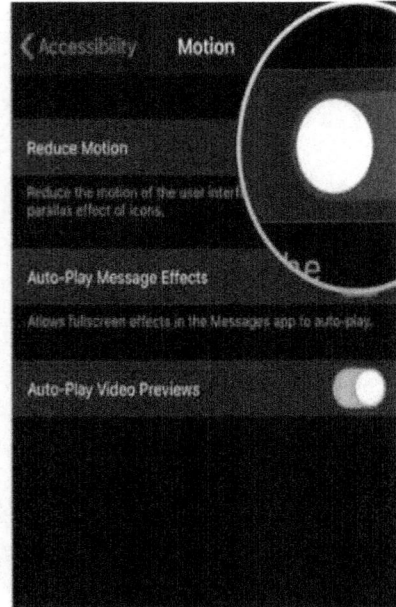

-

Turning off the Lower-case Keyboard
- Open **Settings** and go to **Accessibility**
- Click **Keyboards** under **Physical and motor**
- Click the **button** next to **Show lowercase keys** to turn it to the gray/black "off" position

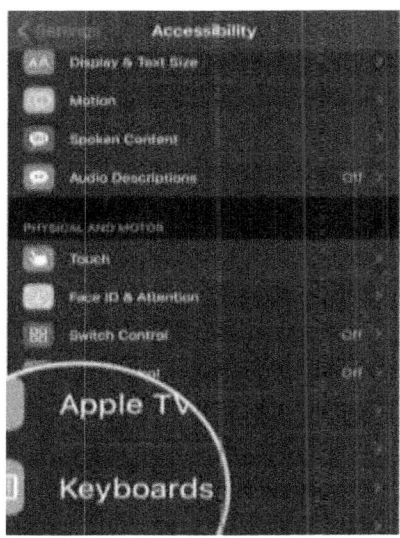
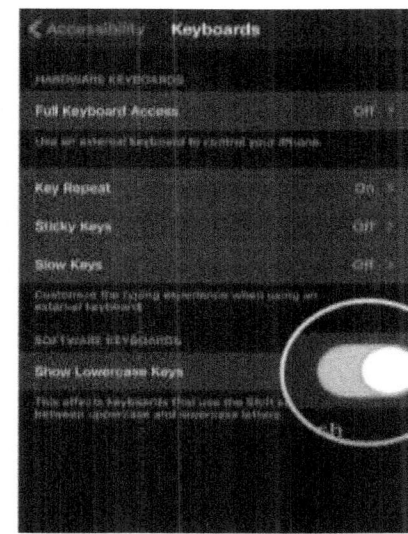

Enabling Character Preview
- Open **Settings**
- Go to **General**
- Next, click on **Keyboard**
- Click the **button** next to **Character preview**

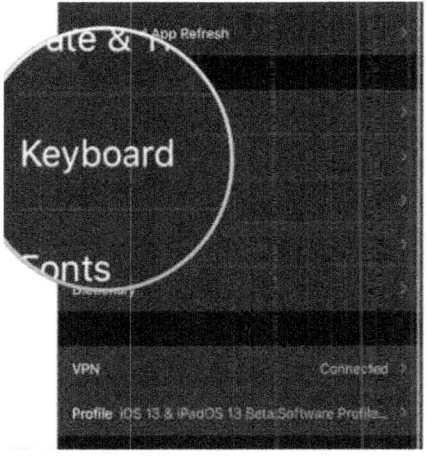
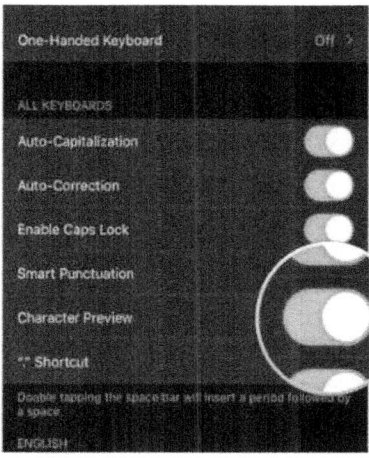

Turning off Reachability
- From **Settings** on your home screen, tap **Accessibility**
- Click **Touch**
- Click the **button** next to **Reachability** so it will be in the gray/black off position

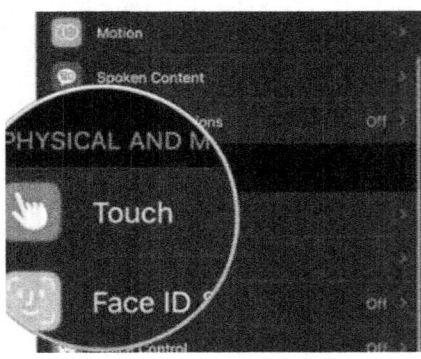 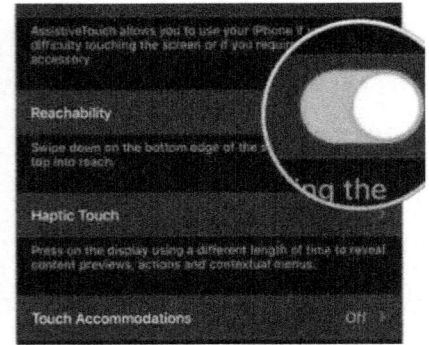

Disabling" Shake to undo"
- Open **settings** and go to **Accessibility**
- Click **Touch**
- Click the **button** next to **Shake to undo** to deactivate it

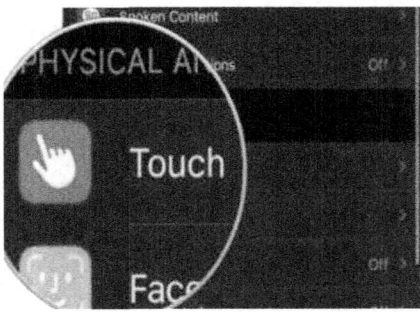 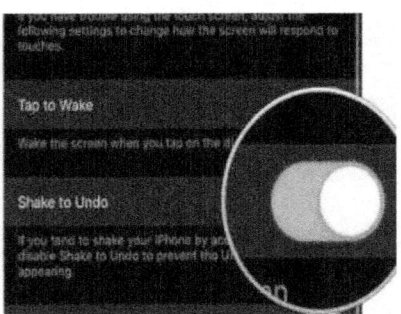

Adjusting the Audio and Information Settings
To turn off lock sounds and keyboard clicks:
- Open **Settings**
- Click on **Sounds & Haptics**

- Navigate down and click on the **buttons** next to **Keyboard clicks** and **Lock sound** to activate or deactivate them

Adjusting the Maps Navigation Volume
- Open **Settings**
- Go to **Maps**
- Click **driving and navigation**
- Choose an option under **Navigation Voice Volume**

Siri Settings
Turning off Siri's voice:

- Open **Settings**
- Click **on Siri & Search**
- Deactivate the **button** for **Listen for "Hey Siri"**

Controlling Siri's Voice Feedback
- Open **Settings**
- Click on **Siri & Search**
- Click on **Voice Feedback**
- Choose from **Always on, Control with Ring switch** or **Handsfree only**

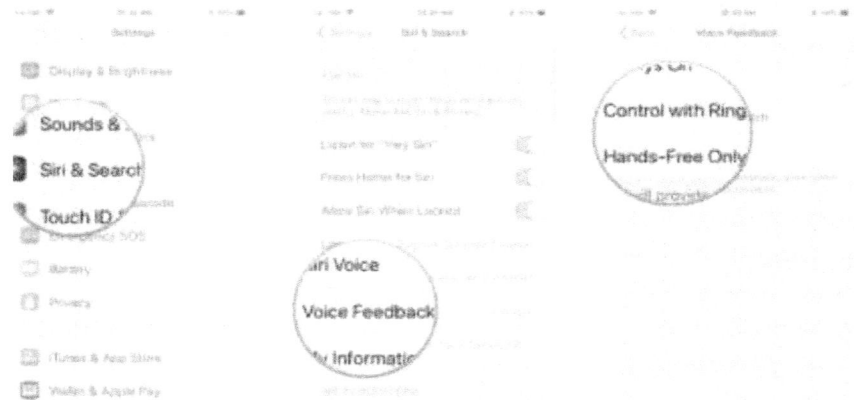

Deactivating Siri Suggestions
- From your screen, **swipe right** to get to Today view
- Next**, swipe up** to navigate down and click the **Edit** button at the bottom

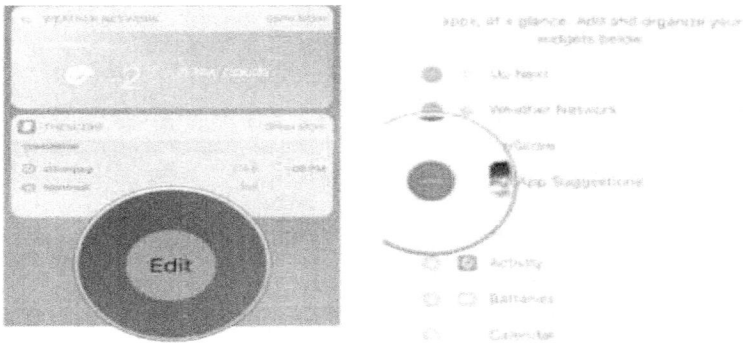

- Click the red circle with the **minus** in the center next to **siri App suggestions**

  - Next, click **remove**

Routing Calls Manually to Speaker or Bluetooth
- Open **Settings** and Click **Accessibility**
- Tap **Touch**
- Navigate down anc click **Call Audio Routing**

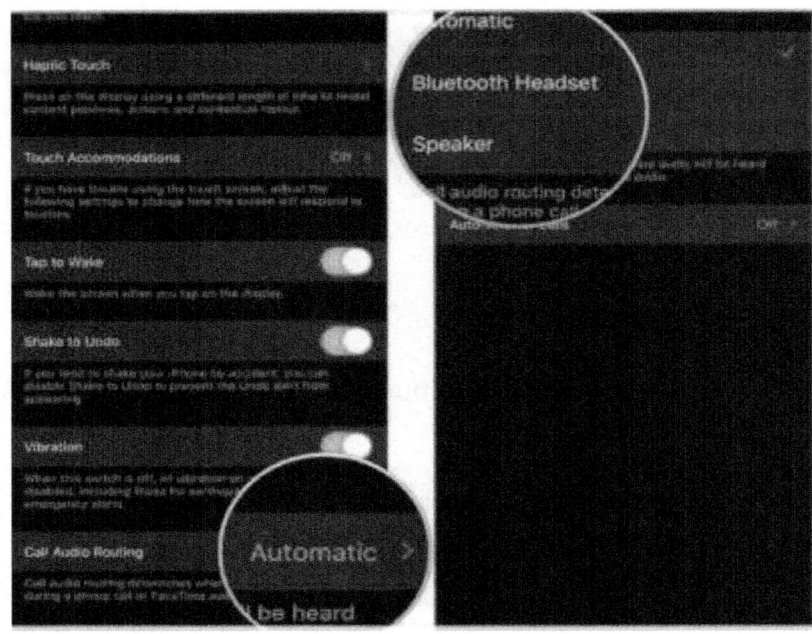

- Click **Bluetooth headset** or **Speaker**

Chapter 10: Taking a screen shot with your iPhone

This is a handy feature for capturing images you ordinarily won't be able to get via normal means of photography or image capturing. It allows you to record virtually anything you can see on your screen.

How to take a Screen Shot:
- Get to the screen that has the **image or App** you want to capture.
- Set it the exact way you desire the shot to be or look like
- Push the **side button and home button** simultaneously as shown below

Viewing and Editing Screen Shots
- Launch the **photos** folder or App

- Click on **Albums**
- Click on **Screenshots**
- Select **Edit**

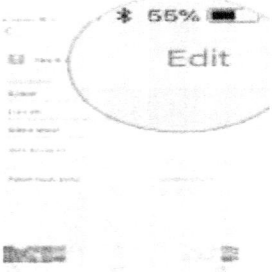

Taking a Screen Shot Using the Assistive Touch Capability of the iphone 12 mini

For users who may not be happy or comfortable with having to push two different buttons simultaneously to take a screen shot, it's possible to take a screen shot using just one simply to press button. Here's how:

- Go to **Settings**

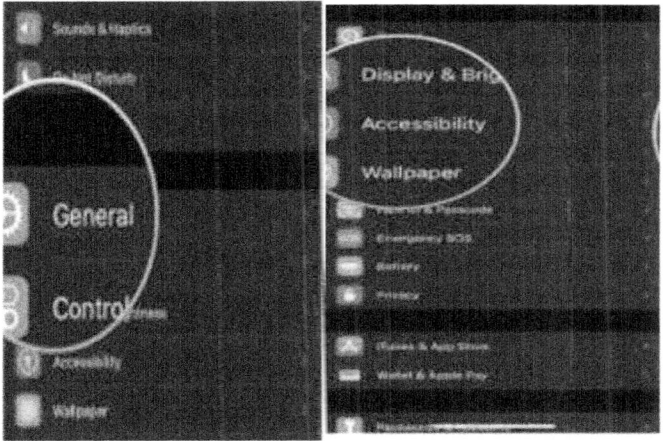

- Go to **General**
- Select **Accessibility**
- Enable the **Assistive touch** button (you will see a semi-transparent button added to the screen)
- Click on the **Customize top Level Menu**
- Next, click on the custom icon (with one star) and select **Screen shot** from the list
- To take a screenshot with the **Assistive touch**, click on the **Assistive button** and then tap the **screen shot** button.

You can replace the screen shot button with any of the default icons at any time you wish.

Chapter 11: Sim settings and operation

The iphone 12 mini is a dual-SIM iPhone that supports two SIMs: one nano SIM card and an eSIM. With ios 14, the two phone numbers can receive and make FaceTime and Voice calls as well as receive and send messages using iMessage, MMS, and SMS. Also, you will be not be able to use two SIMs from two different service providers if using a locked iPhone.

Setting Up Your Cellular Plan

You have several options to activate a cellular plan: you can use your carrier's iPhone app, scan a QR code provided by your supplier, or enter the information manually.

To Scan a QR Code

Use the steps below to activate your cellular plan:

- Go to the **Settings** app on your phone.
- select **Cellular.**
- Select **Add Cellular Plan.**
- Next, use your phone camera to scan the QR code given by the carrier. If asked for a confirmation code to activate the SIM, key in the number provided by your carrier.

Using a service provider App
From the App Store, download the app for your service provider.

- Install the app.
- Next, buy a plan from the app.
- The app will pick the eSIM support on your iPhone.
- obey the guide on your screen to create a new plan.

Entering SIM Information Manually
Follow the steps below to enter your plan manually:

- from **Settings,**
- select **Cellular.**
- Next, click on **Add Cellular Plan.**
- From the bottom of your screen, select **Enter Details Manually.**
- Next, key in the SIM details, for e.g the phone number provided by your service provider.

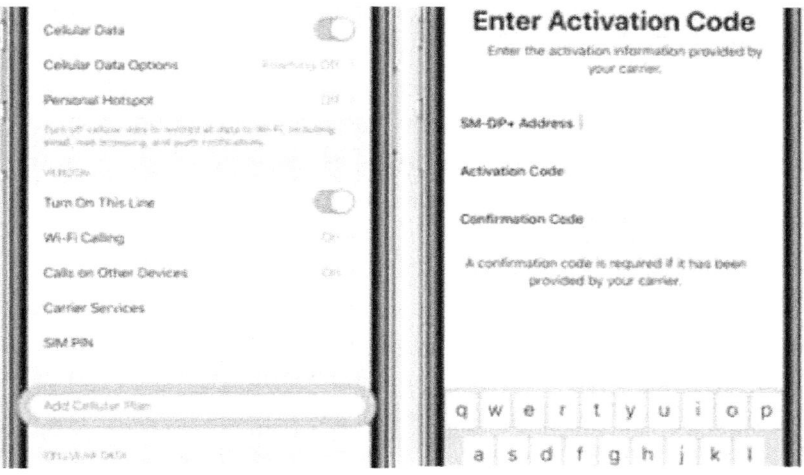

Switch Between SIMs

It's possible for You to have 2 SIMs on your phone but you are only allowed the use of one at any given point in time. To switch between SIMs, find the steps below:

- launch **Settings.**
- select **Cellular.**
- select your preferred SIM.
- Next, select **Turn on This Line.**

Erasing a SIM
- from **Settings,** select **Cellular.**
- select the plan you want to delete.
- Click on **Remove Cellular Plan.**

Labelling Your Plans
- launch **Settings.** Select **Cellular.**
- Select the number you want to label.
- Next, click on **Cellular Plan Label** and choose from one of the default labels, or create a personal label.
- Tap **Done** on your keyboard when you are through.

Setting Your Default Number
- launch **Settings.** Select **Cellular.** Select **Default Line.**
- Choose your preference from the options on your screen.
- **Use (Plan Label) as your default line:** any plan label you choose from here will be used for data, SMS, and voice
- **Use (Plan Label) for cellular only:** this plan is designed for people traveling internationally, who want to use the line for data alone.

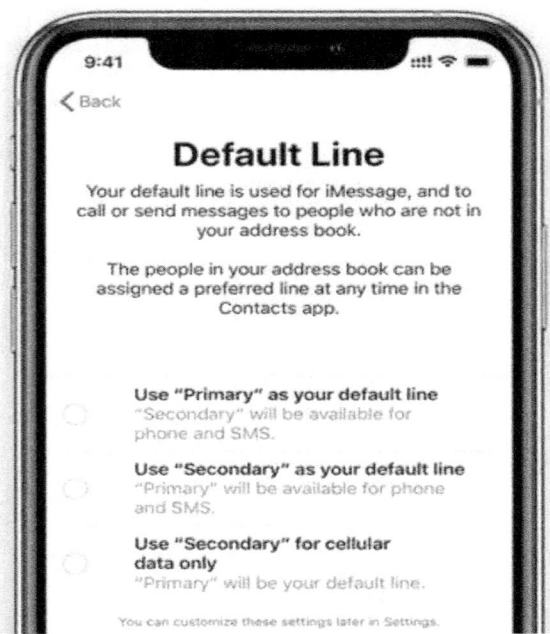

Let Your Phone Remember the Number to Use

To designate the number to use whenever you are calling a contact, do the following:

- Go to the Contacts app and search for the contact.
- Select the contact.
- Click on **Edit** at the top of your screen. Select **Preferred Line.**
- Next, click on the number you want to use for that contact.
- Choose the Number to Use for Call

You can Switch Phone Numbers Before Making a Call with the Steps Below:
- To call the contacts in your Favorite list,

launch the Phone app and select the Favorite tab.

- click (i) beside the contact you want to call
- Tap on the current phone number showing on your screen

83

- Next, click on your second number to call with the other number
- If using the keypad to dial the number
- Key in the recipient's phone number
- Click on the label at the top of the screen

- Then choose the number you want to use.
- Choose Number to Use for a Message

Follow the Steps Below to Choose a Particular Phone Number to Send a Message With:
- Launch the Messages app.
- Click on the **New** button at the top right side of your screen.
- Enter the name of the recipient.
- Click on the label of the current phone number.
- Next, select your preferred number for messaging that contact.

Choosing the Number for Cellular Data

Follow the steps below to assign a number to use for cellular data:

- launch the Settings app.
- Click on **Cellular.**
- Click on **Cellular Data.**
- Then select your preferred number for cellular data.

Allow Cellular Data Switching

Activate **Allow Cellular Data Switching** so that if you are on a voice call on a voice-only phone number, that number will automatically switch to both Voice and Data.

- launch the Settings app.
- Select **Cellular.**
- Click on **Cellular Data.**
- switch on **Allow Cellular Data Switching**

Manage Cellular Settings

Follow the steps below to change the cellular settings for each of your plans:

- Open the **Settings** app. Click on **Cellular.**
- select the **number** you want to change.
- Then select each option and set to your preference.

Chapter 12: iMessaging

It's an instant messaging service that connects Apple users through iPhone, iPad, Mac or Apple watch. Users can send text, picture, video, sound and location.

Before you can start enjoying these features, you need to set up first. Here's how:

If you have enabled iCloud on your iPhone, it's possible that the iMessaging function was activated automatically but if not, follow these steps below:

- Open **Settings**
- Click **Messages**
- Click on the iMessage **On/Off switch.**

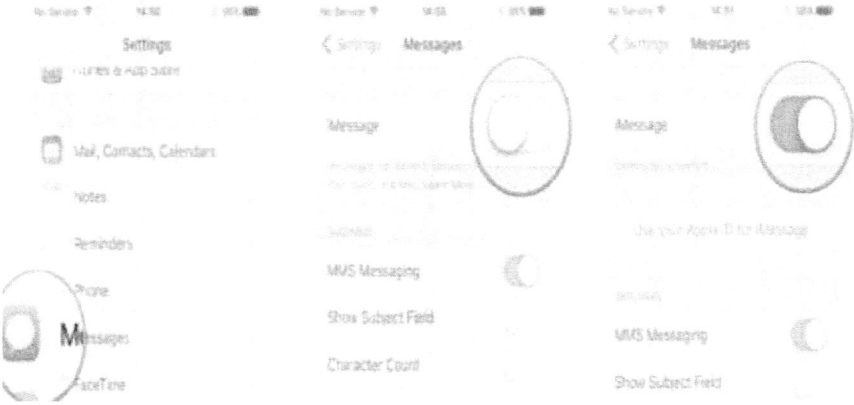

Turning on "Read receipts" on or off in iMessages.
This function is basically used to allow your contacts see if you have seen their iMessages

- Open **Settings**
- Click on **Messages**
- Click on the **Send Read Receipts on/off** switch.

Turning Messages Previews on/off
- Open **Settings**
- Click **Notifications**
- Click **Messages**

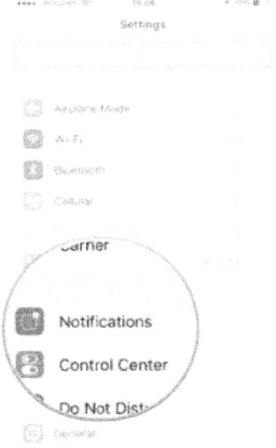

- Click **show previews**
- Next, click on the option you prefer

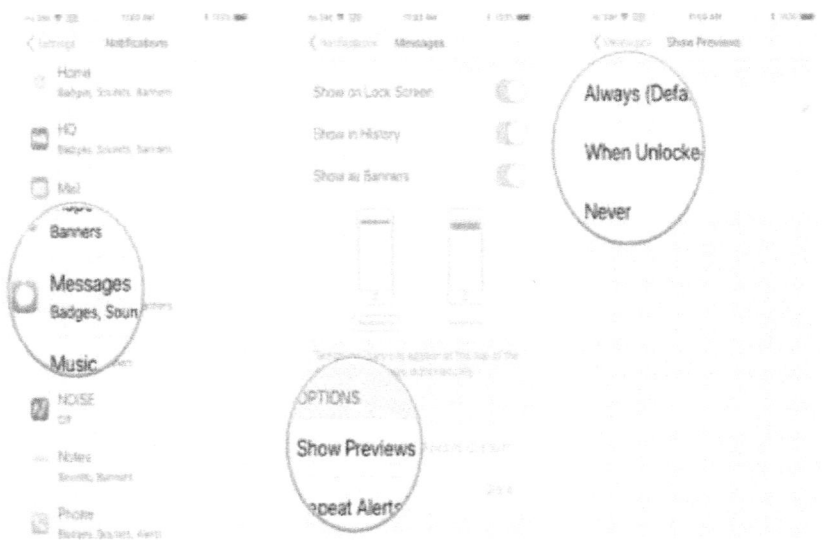

Telling the Difference Between Sending an iMessage or an SMS/MMS

iMessages are contained in a blue bubble and usually work if you are on wi-fi or on cellular data. It works between Apple devices.

SMS/MMS are contained in a green bubble and work with cellular network. It works when messages are sent to other devices that are not Apple devices.

Sending a Text Message via iMessage
- Open **Messages**
- Click **Compose** in the upper right corner of the display screen
- Next, enter the name of the **Recipient**

- Tap out your message in the **message bar or field**
- Click on the **Send** arrow next to the message

Sending a New Photo or Video using Messages
- Open **Messages** and click on the **conversation** in which you would like to send a picture
- Click on the **camera** button to the left of the text field

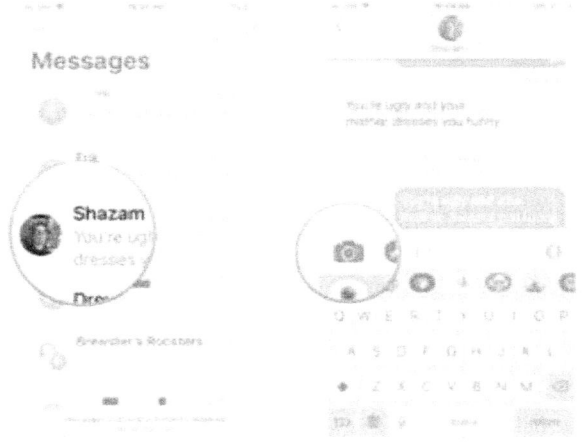

- Click the **shutter button.** You can also swipe right to take a video and wait for a second or two and a new screen will appear.
- You can now **edit** the photo before sending it by tapping the blue **send button** in the right corner at the bottom of the screen.

Sending an Existing Photo or Video via iMessage
- Open **Messages**
- Click on the **conversation** in which you want to send a photo
- Click on the **Apps button** to the left of the text field

- Tap **the Photo Apps button**
- Click the **photo or video** you would like to send

- If you desire, you can add a **comment** and then click on the **blue** send button

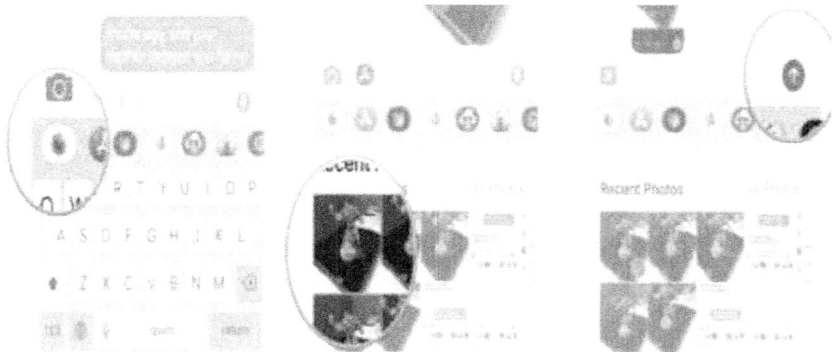

Sending your Current Location Using iMessage

If you want to send someone your current location without having to constantly share your location, here's how you can do it:

- Click on the **name** at the top of the conversation screen in a messages conversation
- Next, click on the **info** button that appears below the name
- Click on **Send My Current Location**

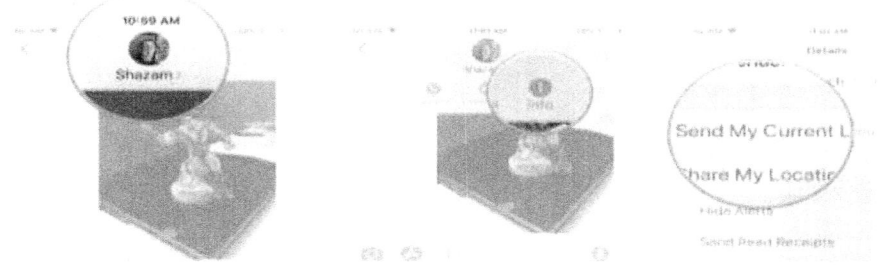

Sharing your Location for a Period of Time

- Open **Messages**
- Click on the chosen **conversation**
- Click on the **name** at the top of the **conversation** screen

- Next, click on the **info** button that appears below the name
- Select **Share My Location**
- Choose the **Duration** for which you would like to share your location

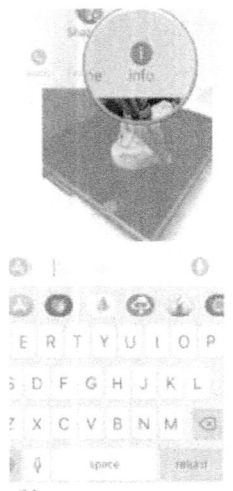
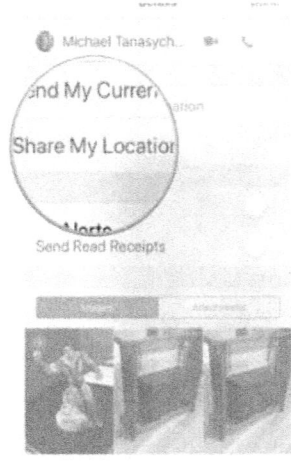

Sharing a Contact Card through iMessages Via the Contacts App
- Open the **Contacts** or **Phone** app
- Locate and click on the **contacts** you would like to share
- Next, tap on **Share Contact** close to the bottom of the screen

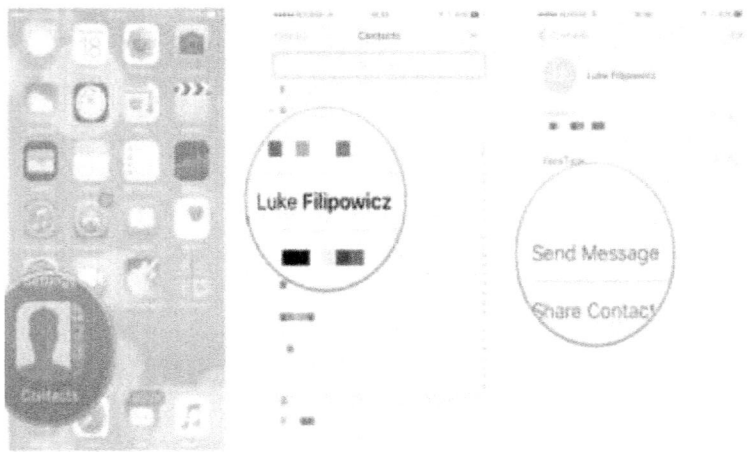

- Click on **Messages** and enter the name of **the Recipient**
- Click on **Send**

Sending your Location from the Maps
- Open the **Maps** app
- Locate the location you would like to share. If it's your current, click on the **location arrow** in order find yourself
- Swipe **up** from the screen bottom
- Next, tap the **Share** button

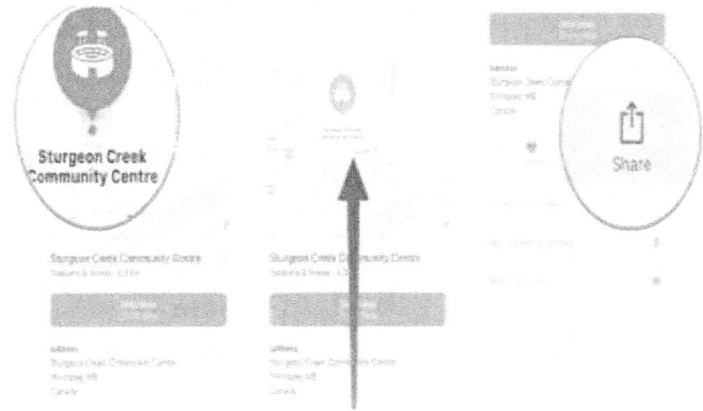

- Click on **Message**
- Enter the **name** of the person that you want to share your location with

- Next, click on **Send**

Sending Messages via iMessage using Siri
- Push and hold the **home button** to launch Siri
- Tell Siri that you want to **send a message,** giving details of the recipient e.g. name, phone number, iMessage linked email address.
- Dictate the **message.**

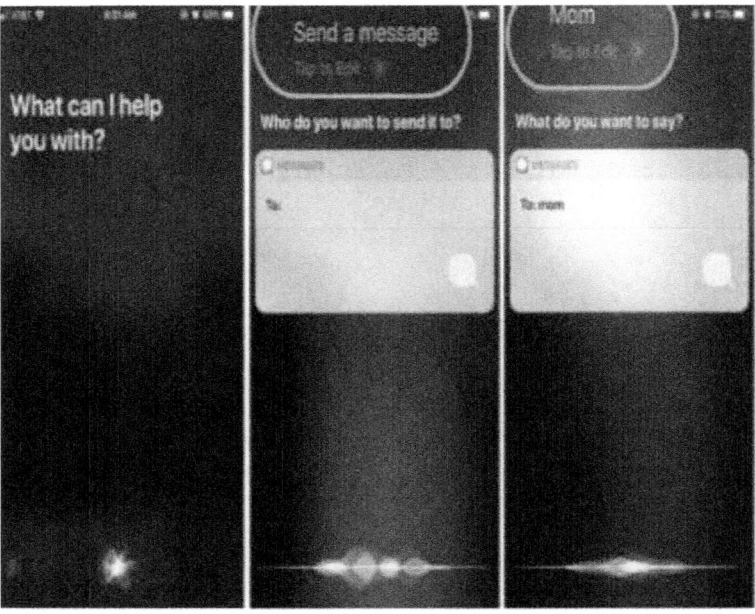

Wait for Siri to **confirm** the content of the dictated text

You can either say or click **Send**

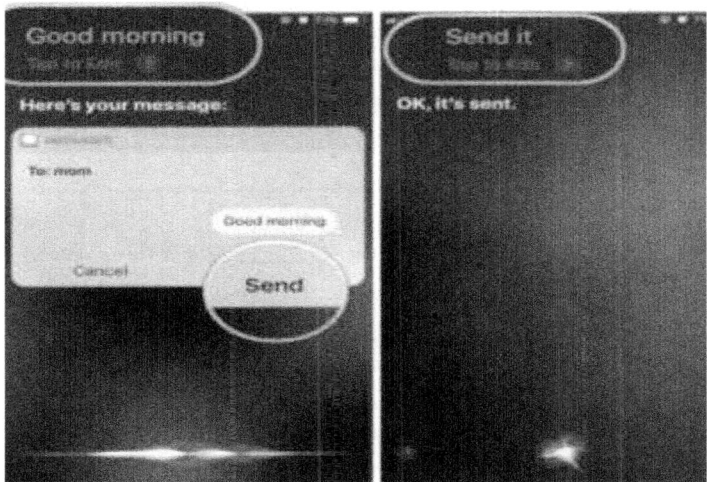

Changing Which Apple ID iMessage Uses on iPhone

Sometimes, it's possible for other people -maybe family members to view messages or content meant for your eyes and it can also go the other way round. This happens because the devices are using the same Apple ID. Here's how to fix this:

The first step is for all those involved to create and have their own unique iCloud account. When this has been done, do the following

- Go to **Settings**. Click **Messages**. Select **Send & receive**

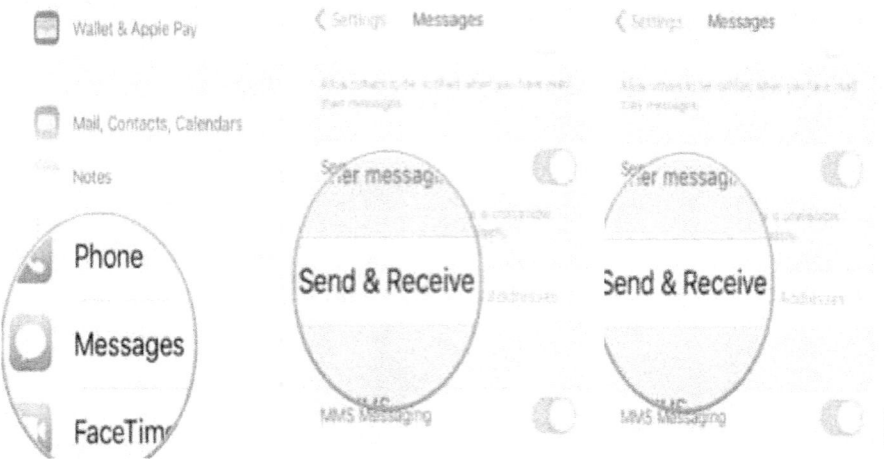

- Click the **Apple ID** at the top of the screen
- Click on **Sign out**

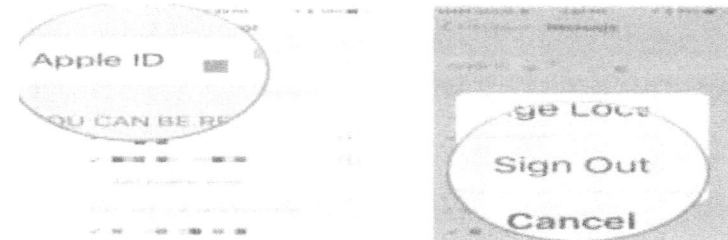

- Select **use your Apple ID for iMessage**
- Use your **Apple ID and password** to log in
- Click **sign in**

Chapter 13: Photos

The photos file of your phone is very handy for storing all the pictures and videos you take or make with your device. you can use the app for a variety of functions such as organizing, sharing and even editing videos or pictures through social media. Here's how to navigate through this very useful tool:

Creating a New Album in the Photos App
- Launch **Photos**
- Click **Albums**
- Click the **+ button** at upper left

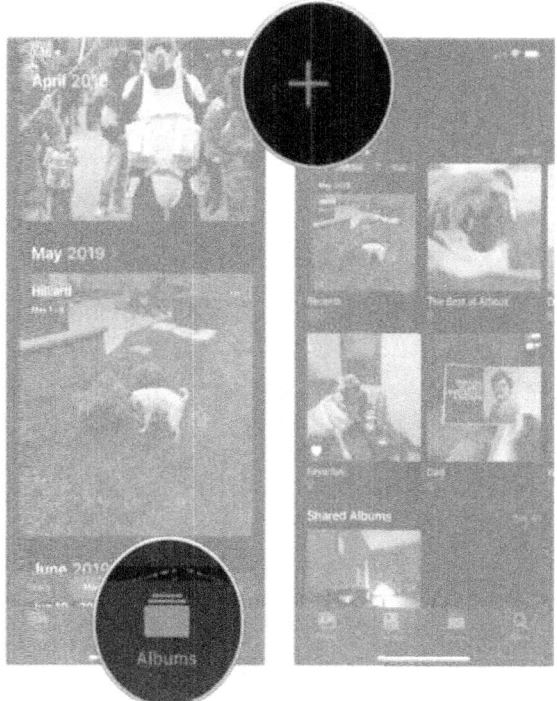

- Click **New Album**
- Give the **Album** a name
- **Save**

  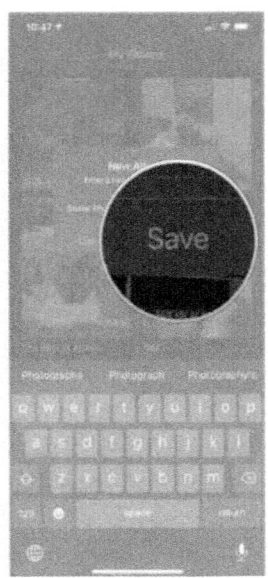

- Select the **photos** you want to include in the Album
- Click **Done**

Creating Shared Albums in the Photos App
- Launch **Photos**
- Click **Albums**

- Click **"+"** at upper left corner

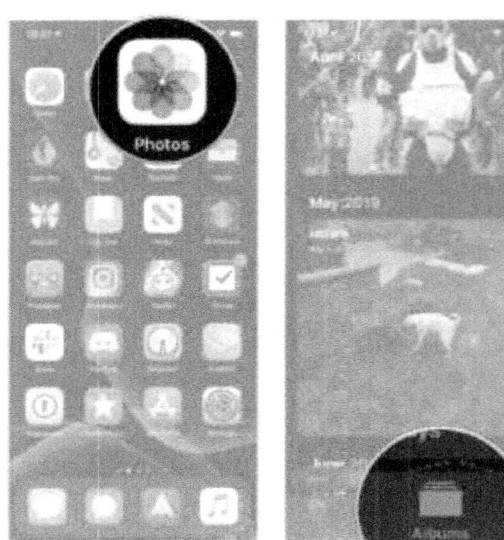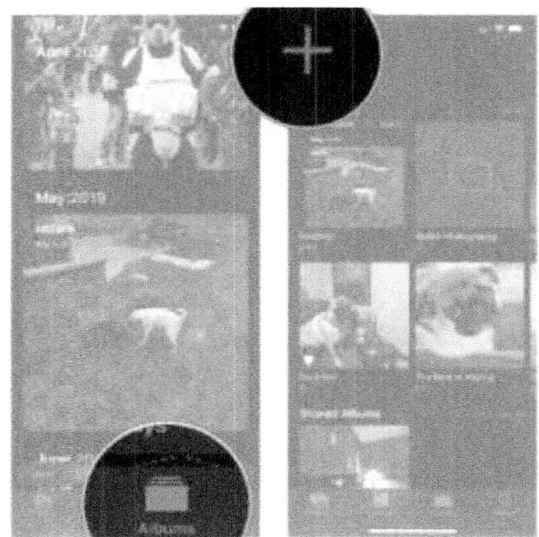

- Click **New Shared Album**
- Give it a **name**
- Click **Next**

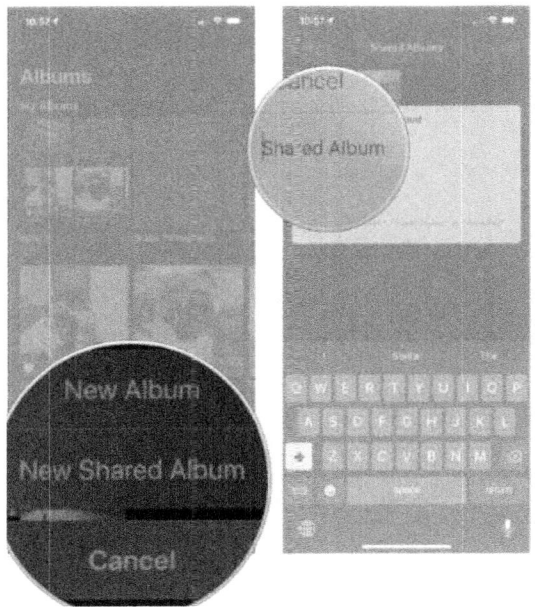

- Type out the **names** of the album recipients
- Click **Create**
- Click the **Shared Album**

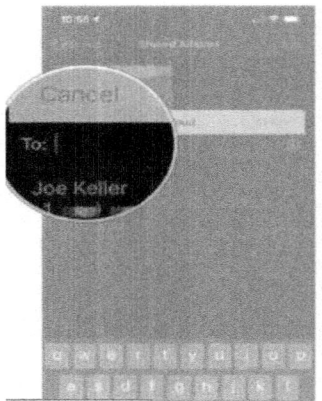

- Click the **+ button**
- Select the **photos** you want to add to the album
- Click **Done**

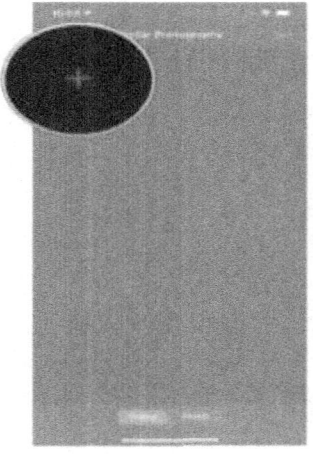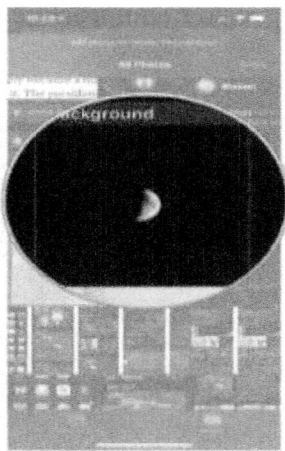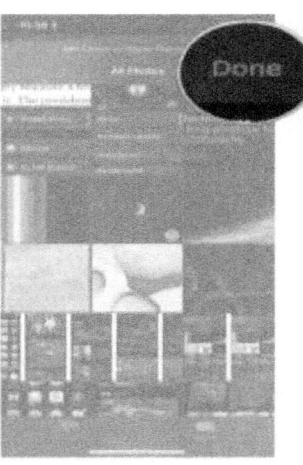

Adding Photos and Videos to Existing Albums in the Photo App
- Launch **Photos**
- Click the **Photos** icon

- Click on either **Days** or **All Photos**

- Click **Select**
- Select the **photos** you would like to add to the album
- Click the **Share** button

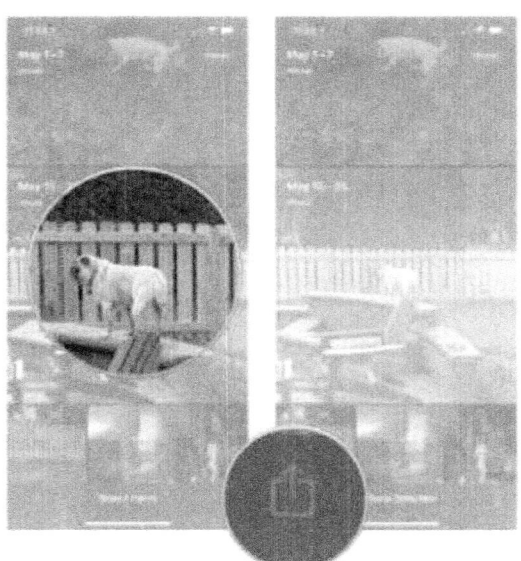

- Select either **Add to Album** or **Add to Shared Album**

- Click on the **Album** that you want to add the photos to

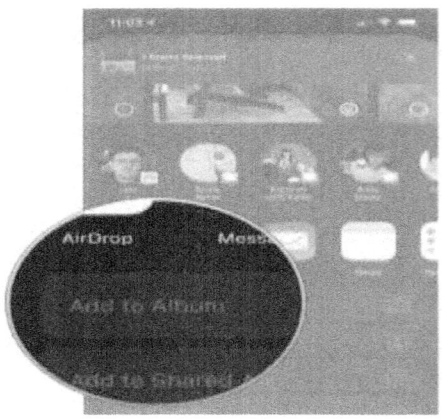
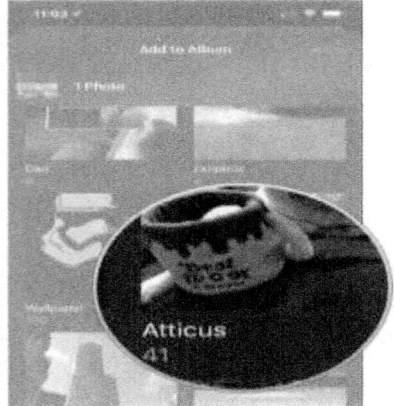

Navigating Between Moments, Collections and Years Smart Groups
- Open **Photos and** click the **back button** to top left of screen. To increase your search scope to days, months and years, just keep going back
- Click on a **photo or video thumbnail** to move to a smaller group

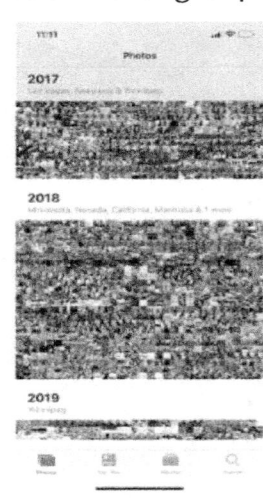

Moving Between Years, Months and Days
- Open **Photos**
- Click on the **Photos** icon

- Next, click on your desired timeline view: **Years, Months, Days** or **All photos**

If you want to back out of any view you are in, just click on the years, months or Days in the menu bar above the tabs for photos

Viewing Picture and Video Locations on a Map
- Open the **Photos** app and click on the **name** of the location above the group of photos which you want a location for
- Swipe upwards to find the **map.** The scrolling might take a little bit of time. Be sure that that you have location services activated beforehand otherwise, you won't be able to view the location of the photos

  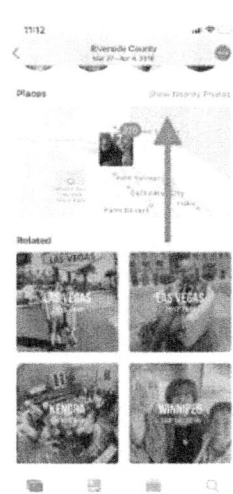

104

Quickly selecting a Month to Jump to from the Years View
- Open **Photos**
- Verify you are in the photos tab that organizes by **Years, Months and Days and** Click on the **Years** view in **Photos**

- Locate the **year** you would like to view
- **Drag** your finger horizontally across the tile
- Click on **collection tile** to jump into the month you left it on while scrubbing

Copying a Video or Picture to the Clipboard in Moments or Albums
- Open the **Photos** app
- Click **Select** to the top right of the screen

- Click the **video** or **photo** you would like to copy

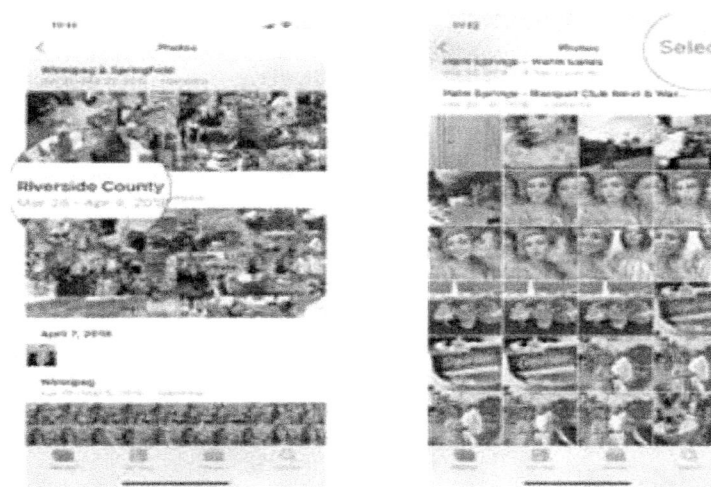

- Click the share button to the bottom left of the screen
- Click copy on the popup menu

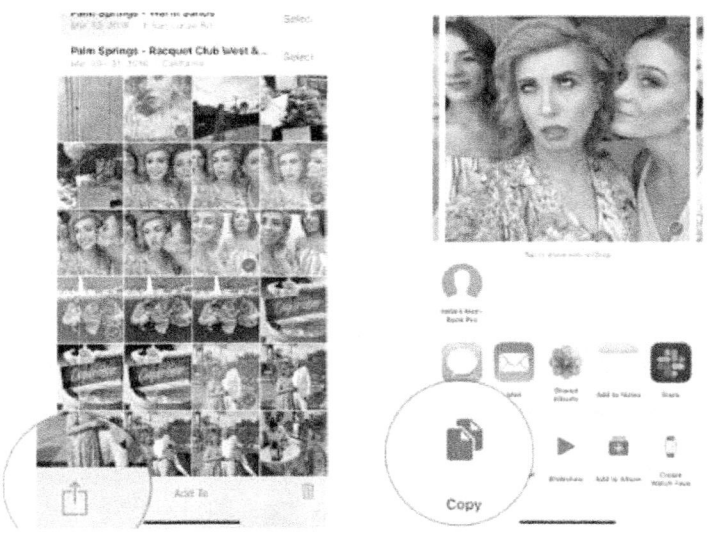

Quickly Copying Pictures or Videos from Moments to the Clipboard
- Open **Photos**
- Go to the **Photos** tab

- Locate the **photos** or **videos** you desire to share from the **All Photos** view
- Click **Select** to top right

 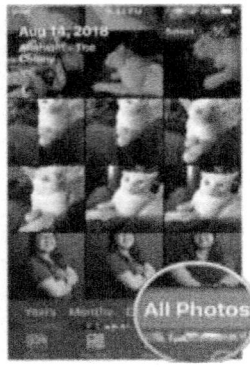 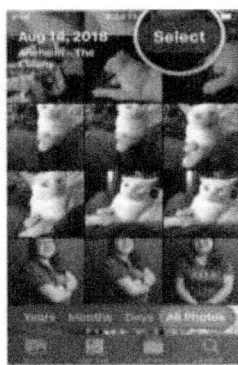

- Select the **photos** or **videos** you want to share or **drag** your finger across rows and columns to quickly select a **batch**
- Click on **Share**
- Navigate down and select **Copy Photos**

 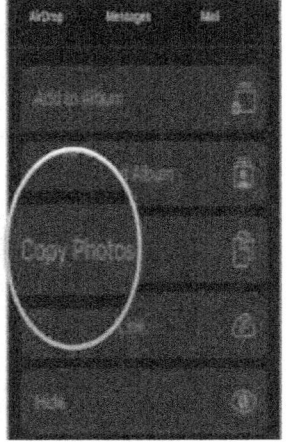

Hiding Images
- Open the **Photos** app

- From the **Days, All photos** or default **Albums** view, click on the **Select** button

  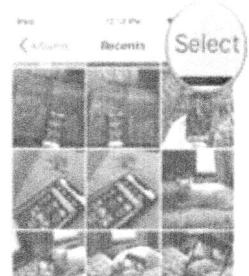

- Select the **photos** you want to hide. It's also possible to hide individual or stand-alone pictures as it is to equally hide a large batch

- Navigate down in the **share sheet**
- **Click on Hide**
- Next, **Confirm** that you want to hide the photos or click **Cancel** if you don't want to hide them anymore

How to Unhide Photos
- Launch the **Photo** app
- Click on **Albums**

- Click on **Hidden Album**
- Click **Select** in the upper corner

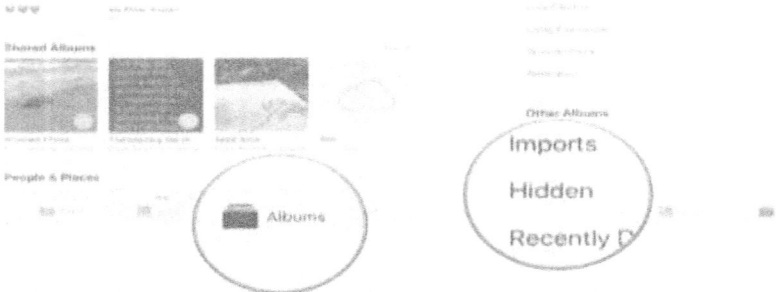

- Select the **photo**s you want to unhide
- From the bottom row of share icons, click **Unhide**

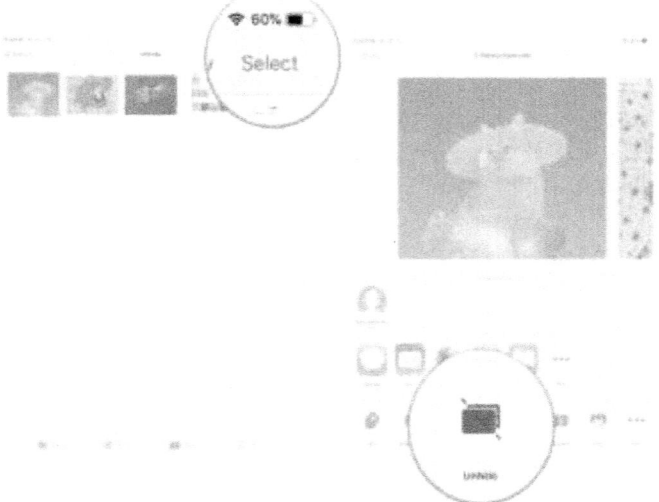

Unhiding Photos or Albums
- Go to **Photos**
- Click **Albums**

- Navigate to the bottom where you will see other **Albums**
- Click **Hidden**
- Click **Select**

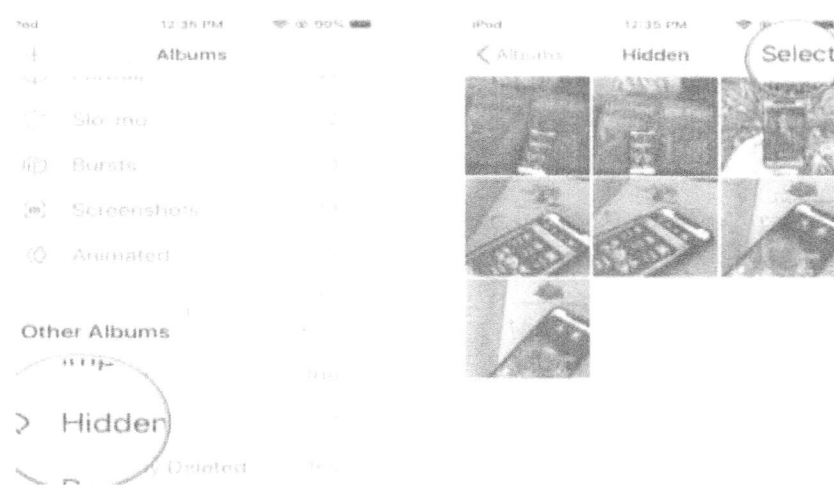

- Select the photos or videos you would want to unhide
- Navigate down and click **Unhide**

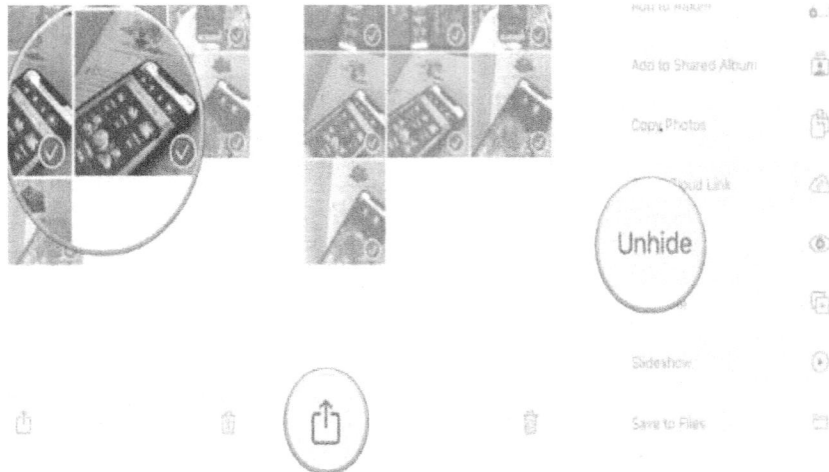

Locating Memories in Photos
- Open the **Photos** app
- Click **Memories** in the menu bar at screen bottom
- Click on a **memory** to view it

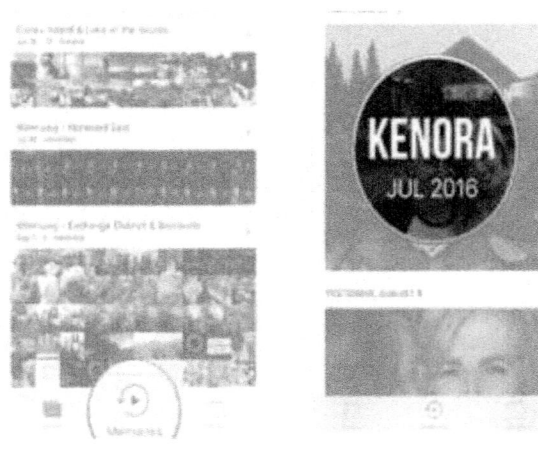

Searching Memories
- Open **Photos**
- Click on **Search** tab

Type the **search terms** you seek to help find a particular memory

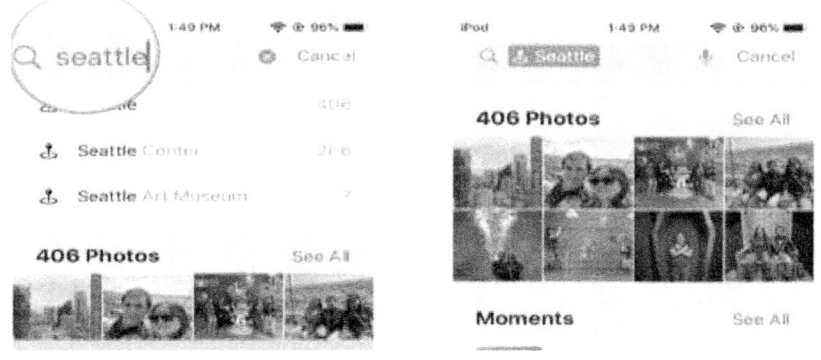

Taking a Photo
- Open the **Camera** app
- Click the **Shutter** button
- Click the **Thumbnail** button to preview and edit

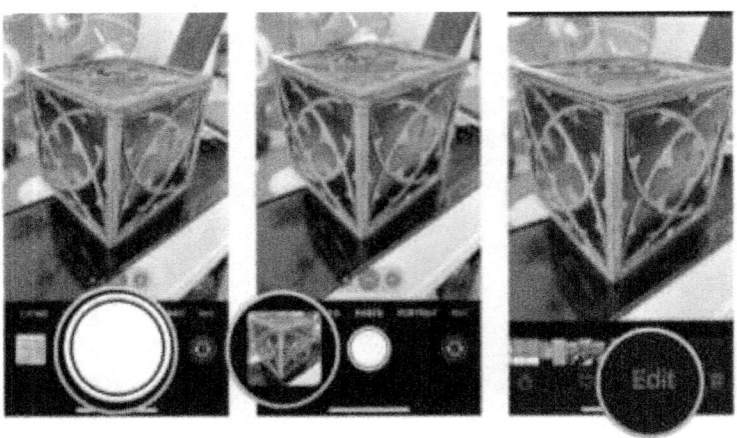

Taking a Burst shot

- Touch and hold the **Shutter Button**. When you are done, lift your finger from the shutter button
- Tap the burst thumbnail and tap **Select** to choose pictures to keep
- To save any photo as individual photo, tap the circle at lower right corner and tap **Done**

Taking a Live Photo

With the live photo setting, you can capture what happens before and after you take the shot.

- Select photo mode
- Tap ◉ to turn Live Photos on and off
- Tap the shutter button to shoot

Recording a Video

- Select **video** mode
- Next, tap the **record button** or press any of the **volume buttons** to start recording
- When you finish tap either the **record button** or any of the **volume buttons**

Recording a Quick Take Video
You can record videos while in photo setting or mode. You can also lock the record button and continue taking photos while you record

- From photo setting, **touch and hold** the **shutter button** to start recording a QuickTake video. You can also do it by **pressing and holding** any of the **volume buttons**
- Next **slide the Shutter button** to the right and let go over the lock for hands-free recording
- The record and shutter buttons show below the frame. Tap the **shutter button** to take photos while recording
- When you finish, tap the **Record button** to stop

Recording a Slow-Motion Video
- Select **Slo-mo** setting
- Next tap the **Record button** or **press and hold** any **Volume button** to begin recording
- You can still take photos by tapping the **shutter button**
- To end the recording, tap the **record button** or any of the **volume buttons**

Playing a Portion of Recorded Video in Slow Motion
- Tap the **video thumbnail**. Tap **Edit. Slide the vertical bars** below the frame viewer to highlight the section to be played in slow motion

Changing the Slow-Motion Recording Settings
- Launch S**ettings**. Tap **Camera**. Tap **Record Slo-mo**.

Capturing a Time-Lapse Video
- Select **Time-Lapse** mode
- Set up the phone where you want to capture a moving scene
- Tap the **record button** to begin and tap it again to end when you finish

Using Quick Toggles to Change Video Resolution and Frame Rate
- Tap the **toggles at top right** to switch between HD or 4K recording and 24, 30 or 60 frames per second
- To display quick toggles, launch **Settings**. Tap **Camera**. Tap **Record Video**. Turn on **Video Format Control**

Setting the Flash
- Open the **Camera** app
- Click the **flash icon** in the upper left corner
- Choose if you want it on **Auto, On** or **Off**

Setting the Timer
- Open the **Camera** app
- Tap the **arrow** at screen top or **swipe up** from above the shutter button

 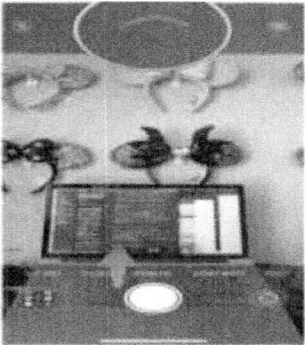

- Click the **timer** button
- Choose between **3 seconds** or **10 seconds**
- Next click the **shutter button** to begin the countdown. The screen should start blinking as it counts down.

 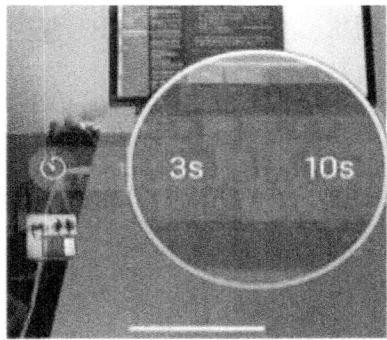

Switching in Between Cameras (front and rear facing)
- Open the **Camera** app
- Click the **flip camera button** to alternate between the front facing facetime and rear camera
- Next click the **shutter button** to shoot picture or start recorcing a video

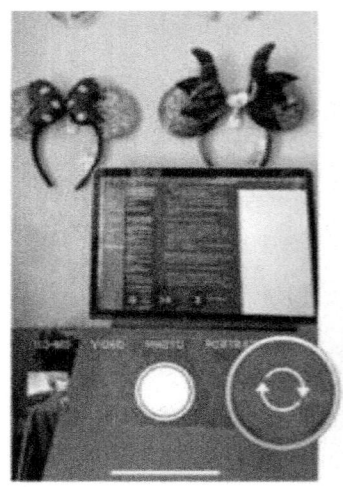 

How to take a Square Photo
- Open the **camera** app
- Click on the **arrow** at screen top or **swipe up** from above the shutter button

- Next, click on the **aspect ratio** button
- Click on **square**

How to take a Panorama

- Open the **Photo** app
- Swipe to the **left twice** to change the mode to pano
- Click the **arrow** button to change the capture direction

- Click the **shutter button** to begin taking a panoramic photo
- **Turn your device** to capture as much of your environment to your desire.
- To finish, click the **shutter button** again

Enhancing Images in Photos
- Open the **Photos** app
- Locate the photo you want to enhance and open it
- Click on the **Edit** button in the upper right corner of the screen
- Click on the **auto-enhance button** that has the appearance of a magic wand
- You can switch between Auto-Enhance by clicking on it again to let you see before and after
- Click **Done** if you like the adjustments the Auto-Enhance feature made

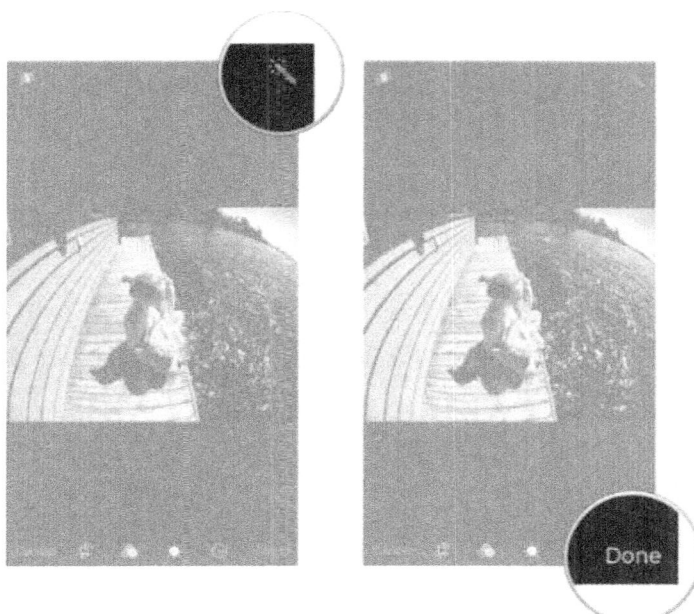

How to Enhance Photos

- Open **photos**
- Locate a photo to enhance and open it

- Click **Edit** at upper right corner
- Ensure you are in the **lighting** section (a dial with dots around it) and click the **auto-enhance** button that resembles a magic wand

- You can slide the **dial** at the bottom to change the intensity of the **auto-enhance** feature. This makes changes to other aspects automatically
- Click **Done** in the bottom right corner when you finish

Changing Lighting with Smart Adjustments in Photos
- Open the **photos** app
- Locate the **photo** you would like to enhance and open it

- Click on the **Edit** button at the upper right of the screen
- Click on the **adjustments** button that looks like a dial with dots around it at the bottom navigation.
- Click on **Light**
- Swipe left and right to move the **slider** to effect adjustments to your photo

- Click and hold on the **photo** to see the original so you can view it in comparison to your edited version
- Click **Done** at bottom right and your changes will be saved

Changing the lighting in your photos

- Open **Photos**
- Locate a **Photo** and open it
- Click **Edit** in upper right corner
- Click the **Lighting** button in the bottom menu bar
- **Swipe horizontally** to browse the various categories and click the one you want to adjust

For each adjustment you want to do, slide the **dial** at the bottom left to right for a more pronounced or less pronounced effect

- Click **Done** at bottom right corner to **save** the changes you have made

Changing Color in your Photos
- Open **photos**
- Locate the photo you want to work on and open it

- Click the **Edit** Button
- Click on the **color** button at the center of the bottom menu bar
- **Swipe** left and right to find a color filter that you like

- If you need to make further adjustments to color, click on the **lighting** button at bottom menu bar
- Choose between **Saturation, Vibrance, Warmth** and **Tint** by **swiping** left and right
- Adjust the **dial** till you are ok
- Click **Done** at bottom right to **save**

Converting Photos to Black and White
- Open **photos**
- Locate the photo and open it

- Click the **Edit** button
- Click the **color** button in the bottom menu bar
- Swipe through the filters till you get to the 3 options: **Mono, Silvertone** and **Noir**. As you click through, they are automatically applied

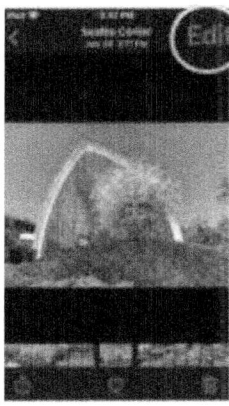  

- If you feel the need to make any adjustments, click on the **lighting** button to make any changes to the lighting aspect
- Click **Done** to **save**

Fine-tuning with Smart Adjustments in Photos
- Open **Photos**
- **Locate and open the photo**
- Click on the **Edit** button at screen upper right
- Click on the **adjustments** button in the bottom navigation
- Click on the **dropdown arrow** next to **Color, Light,** or **B&W**
- Click the **name of the adjustment** you would like to make

- Use the **slider** to swipe left and right to make an adjustment
- Click and hold the photo to see the **original** to compare to the edited one
- Click **Done** at bottom right corner and **save** changes

Reverting to Original Photo
- Open **Photos**
- Locate an edited photo
- Click **Edit** at upper right corner
- Click **Revert** at bottom right
- Next, **confirm** that you want the **edited** photo rest restored to **original** form

  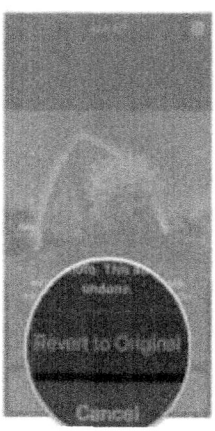

Trimming your video

- Open **Photos and** select **Albums** at bottom of the app

- Click **Videos**
- Select the **video** you want to edit
- Click **Edit** at top right of the screen

- Click and hold on the left or right side of the **timeline** to activate the trimming tool
- Move the **anchor** left or right to trim

- Click on and hold an anchor to expand the **timeline** for more accurate editing
- Click **Done** at bottom right of screen

Resizing a Video
- Open **Photos**
- Go to **Albums** at app bottom
- Select **Videos**
- Choose the **video** to edit
- Click **Edit** at top right of screen
- Click on the **crop** icon
- Using your finger, choose from **Straighten, Horizontal, or Vertical**

Move your finger left or right to resize

Flipping and Rotating a Video
- Open **photos.** Go to **Albums.** Select the **video** to edit
- Click **Edit** at top right of screen
- Click on the **crop** icon
- Select the **flip** icon at top left to flip the video
- Click the r**otate** icon at top left to rotate the video.
- Click **Done**

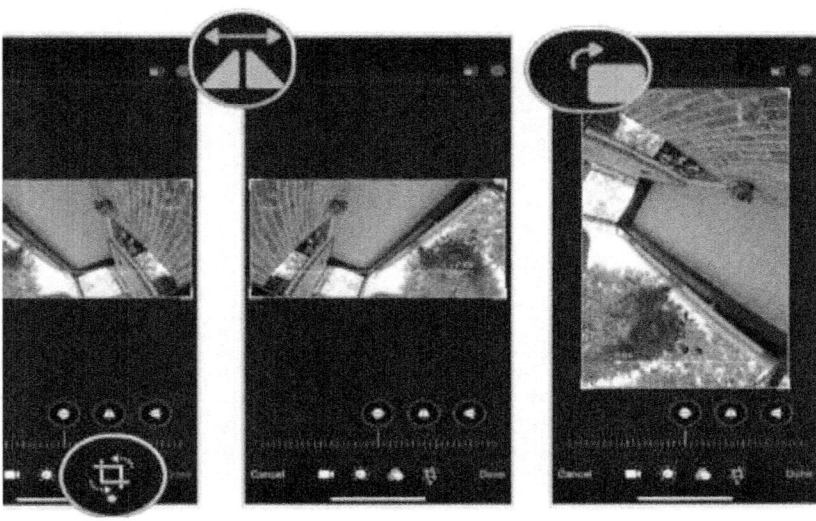

Adjusting the Video Brightness
- Open **Photos.** Go to **Albums.** Select **Videos**
- Choose the **video** to edit and click **Edit** at top right of screen
- Click on the **adjustment** icon and select the **brightness** circle
- You can move left and right to select a **brightness level**
- Click **Done**

 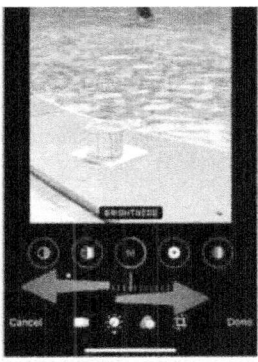 

Adding a Video Filter
- Open **photos.** Go to **Albums.** Select **Videos**
- Choose the **video** to edit
- Click **Edit** at top right
- Click on the **filter** icon
- From under, move left and right to change the **filter setting**
- Click **Done**

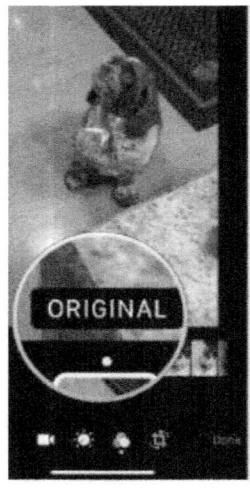  

Muting video Sounds
- Open **photos**. Go to **Albums**. Select **videos**
- Choose the **video** to edit
- Click **Edit** at top right
- Click the **sound** icon at the top left to turn it on or off
- Click **Done**

Using Filters in the Photos App
- Open **photos**

- Click on the **photo** to apply filter
- Click **Edit** button at top right of screen

 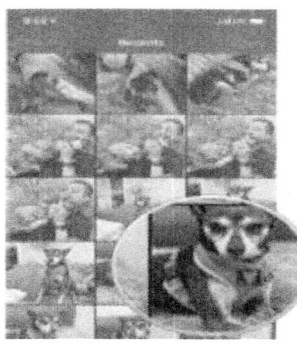 

- Click the **filters** button at middle of bottom menu
- Move and click on the **filter** you want to apply
- Click **Done**

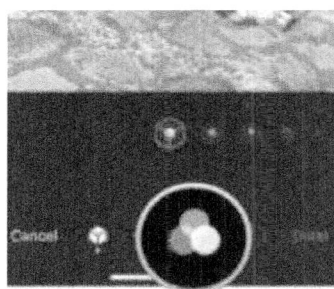 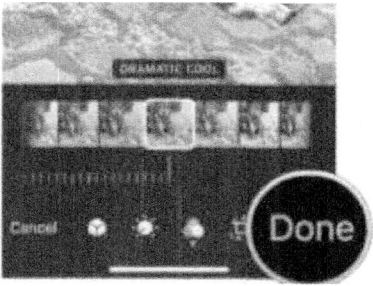

Rotating Photos
- Open **photos**
- Find and open the **photo**
- Click on **Edit** at top right corner
- Click on the **crop** button at bottom menu

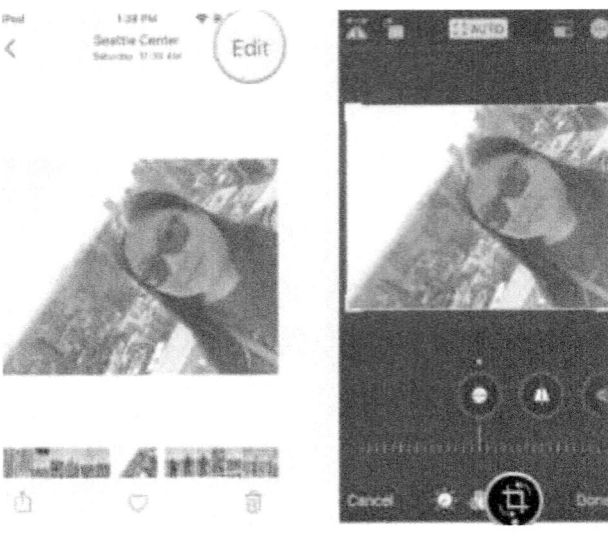

- The **rotate** button looks like a box with a curved arrow. Click on it to rotate the photo till you get your desired alignment
- Click **Done** to save changes

To Straighten Photos

- Open **Photos**
- Find and open a **photo**
- Click **Edit** at upper right corner
- Next, click the **crop** button at bottom menu

Normally, it goes to **straighten**. Drag you finger along the dial at bottom to straighten out the image

You can still click on the **Vertical** or **Horizontal** options if you want the photo in any of those alignments

- Adjust the **slider** till you are happy with the results
- Click **Done** to save changes

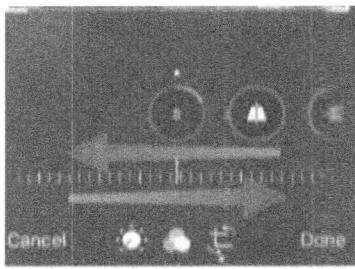
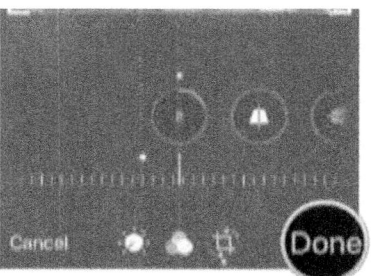

Cropping Photos
- Open **Photos**
- Find and open the **photo**
- Click **Edit** in upper right corner
- Click the **crop** button at bottom menu

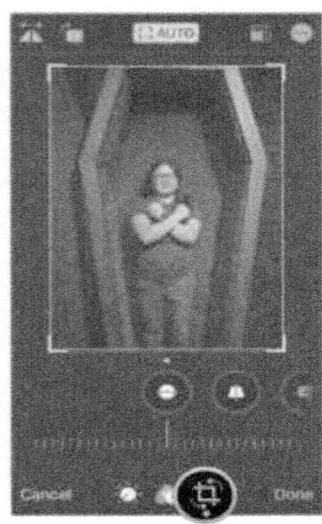

- Click and drag on the **corner handles** of the crop till you are happy with the results
- Click **Done** to save changes

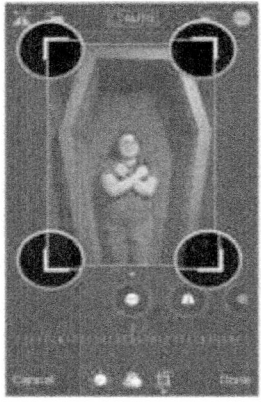
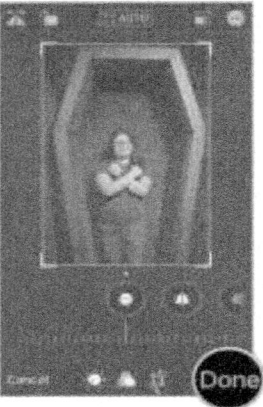

Changing the Aspect Ratio in Photos
- Open **Photos**
- Find and open the **photo**
- Click **Edit** at top right of the screen
- Click on the **crop** icon at bottom menu
- Next, click on the **aspect ratio** button at lower right of screen

- Move your finger on the **dial** to center the photo to your liking
- Click **Done** when you are done

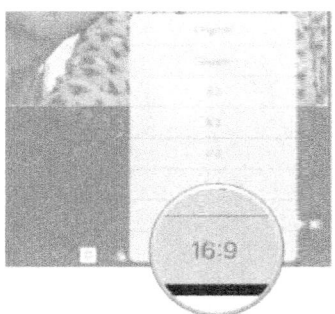 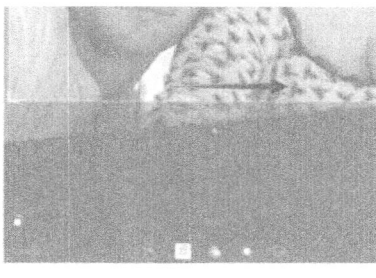

Turning on Photo and Video Extensions in Photos in the Photo app
- Open the **Photos** app
- Click on the photo or video you want to edit
- Click **Edit** at upper right corner

- Click on the **"..."** button at upper right corner
- Click on **More** in the menu

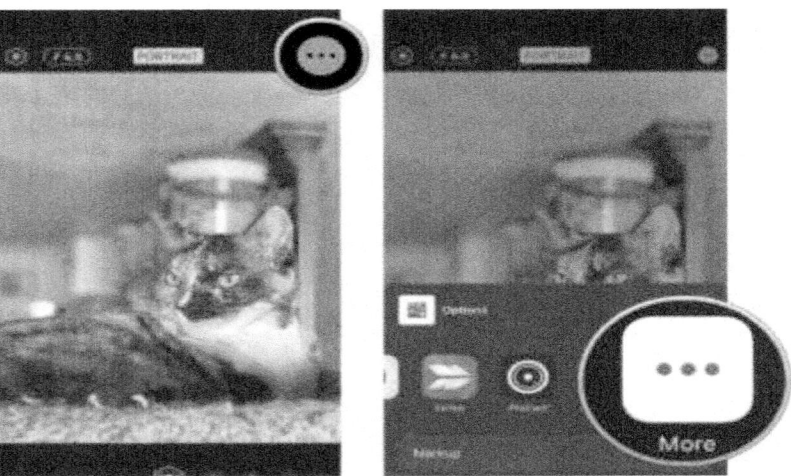

- Click on **Edit**
- Next, click the **green circle with a white cross in the middle** on the extensions you want to favorite and you can rearrange the order they appear by moving the handle on the right

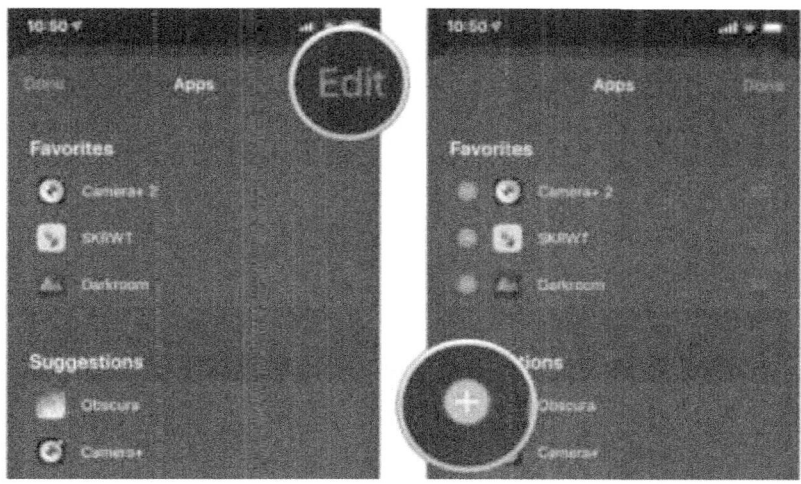

Accessing and Using Photo and Video Extensions in the Photos app
- Follow steps 1-4 as outlined in how to turn on photo and video extensions in photos app above
- Next, tap on the **extension** you want to use
- Do your editing
- Click **Done** to save changes

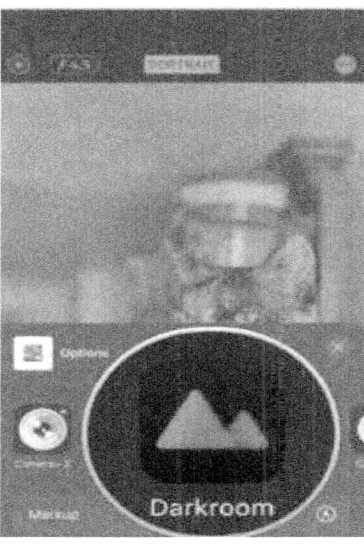 

Assigning Pictures to Contacts Via the Photo App
- Open the **Photos** app
- Click the **album** that contains the photo you want to use for your contacts photo
- Click on the specific photo and open it
- Next, click on the **Share** button at bottom left corner

- Locate and click **Assign to contact** on bottom menu
- Click on the **contact** that you would like to assign the photo to

- Set the **scale** of the photo you want to use to ensure it fits the frame
- Click **Update** to save changes

 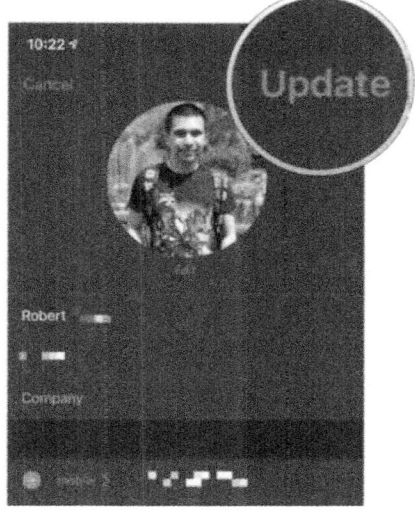

Using the Photo App to set Your Wall paper
- Open **the Photo** app
- Open the **album** you would like to use in the slideshow
- Click on and open the **photo** you would like to use to open it

- Click on the **Share** button at bottom left corner
- Locate and click **Use as Wallpaper** at bottom menu

- Click **Set** and choose the screen to which you would apply the wallpaper. You can choose **Set Lock screen, Set Home Screen** or **click** on **Set Both**

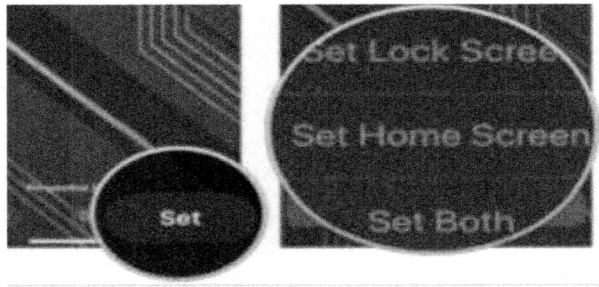

Starting a Slideshow with the Photos App
- Open **Photos**
- Click on an **album** or the **photos** icon
- Click **Select**
- Select the **photos** you want in your slideshow
- Click the **Share** button at bottom left
- Click on **Slideshow**. It should start at once

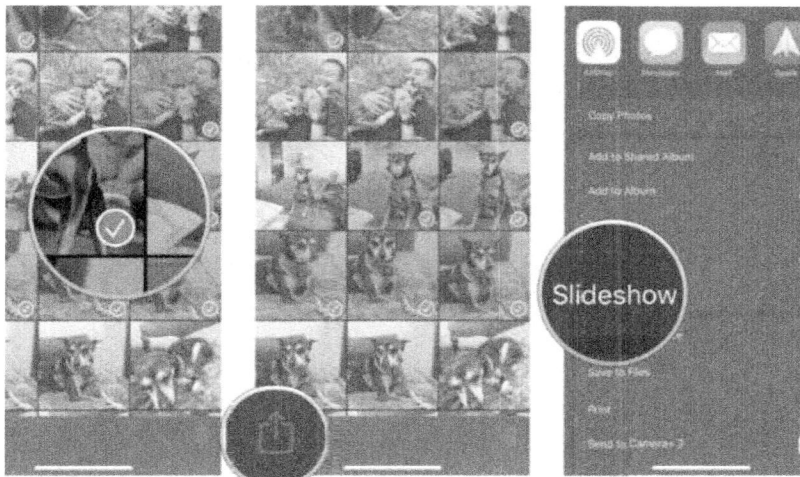

Playing a Whole Album as a Slide Show
- Open **Photos**
- Click the **album** you want to play as a slide show

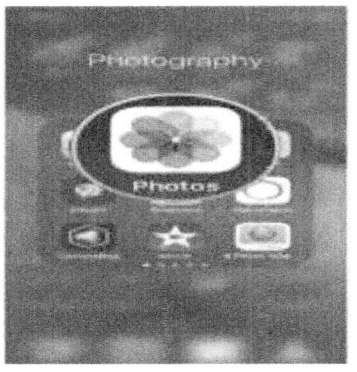 

- Click the **album** name and **date range**
- Click on the **play** button

Airplaying Your photos to Your TV

- Open the **Photos** app

- Click on the **photo** or **video** you want to share

- Click on the **Share** button at bottom left corner

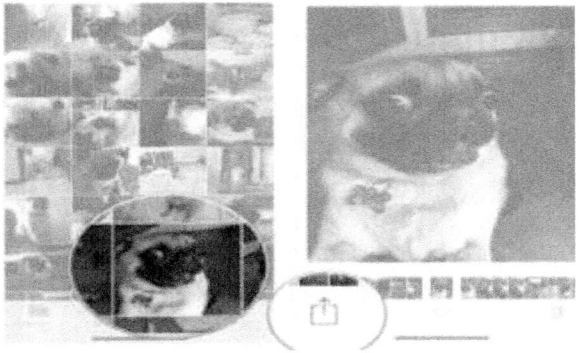

- Click **Airplay**

- Next, click on the **Apple TV** or **Airplay-compatible Tv** to which you would like to share the photo or video

Sharing Individual Photos or Videos Using Photos
- Open the **Photos** app
- Click on the **photo** or **video** you want to share
- Click on the **Share** button at bottom left corner
- Click on the sharing **method**

sharing individual photos or videos
- Open **Photos**
- Locate a specific **photo** or **video** to share
- Click on the **Share** button at bottom right
- Choose the sharing method

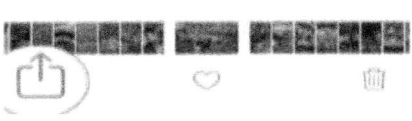

Sharing Multiple Photos
- Open **Photos**

- Find the **photos** or **videos** to share
- Click **Select** at top right

- Click on the **photos** or videos to share. In the alternative, you can drag your fingers across rows and columns for faster selection
- Click **Share**
- Choose your sharing method

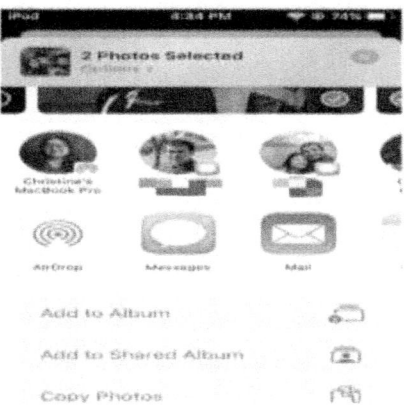

Printing Photos
- Open **Photos**

147

- Click on the **photo** you want to print
- Click on the **Share** button at lower left corner

- **Swipe** to the left from the bottom menu to view the **print** option
- Next, click on **Print**
- Click **Select Printer**

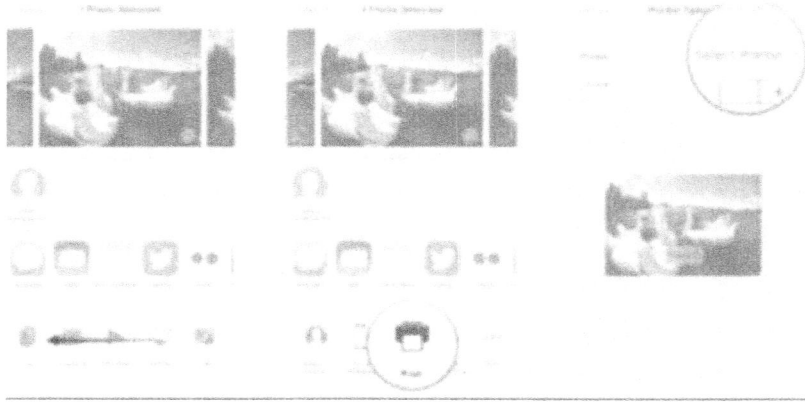

- Click on the specific **printer** you want to use
- Use the **+ or −** buttons to specify the number of copies
- Click **Print**

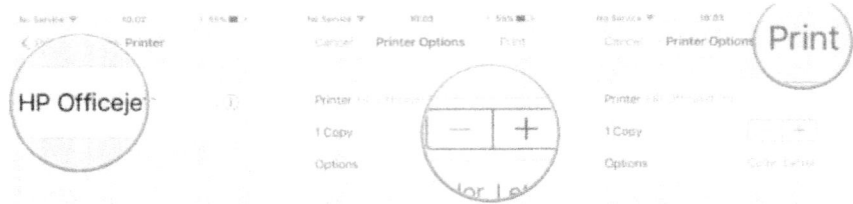

Using Siri to Locate Photos Based on Time

Push **the Home** or **Side button** to activate siri or you can say **"Hey Siri"**

You can say something like: **"show me photos from March"**

You can choose to be more **specific** by mentioning a **particular date** not just month for better accuracy

Using Siri to Find Photos Based on Location

Push and hold the **Home** or **Side button** to activate **siri or say "Hey Siri"**

You can now say something like **"show me photos from California"**

Using Siri to Find Photos of Things

Press and hold the **Home** or **side button** to activate Siri or you can say

"Hey siri"

You can now say something like, **"show me photos of airplanes"**

Searching for Photos in the Photos App

- Open the **Photo**s app
- Click the **Search** icon at bottom right corner
- From the search screen you can choose to search the following:
- **Moments, People, Places, Categories** and **Groups**

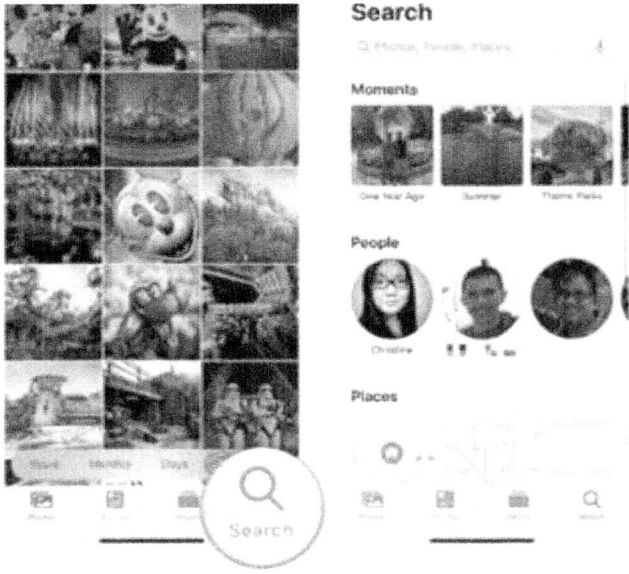

Using the Search Bar to Find What you Want in the Photos App
- Click the **Search Bar** at the top of the Search section
- **Enter** the keywords you want to search for
- Click **Search** on the keyboard when Done

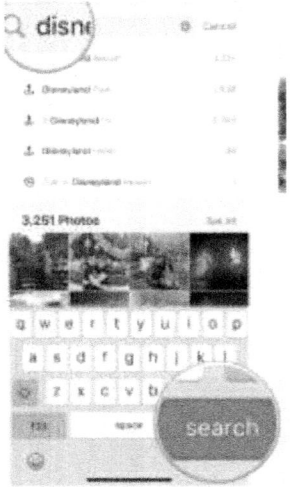

Using Names to Make People Easier to Locate in the Photos App
- Open **Photos**
- Click **Albums**
- Navigate down and select the people **album**

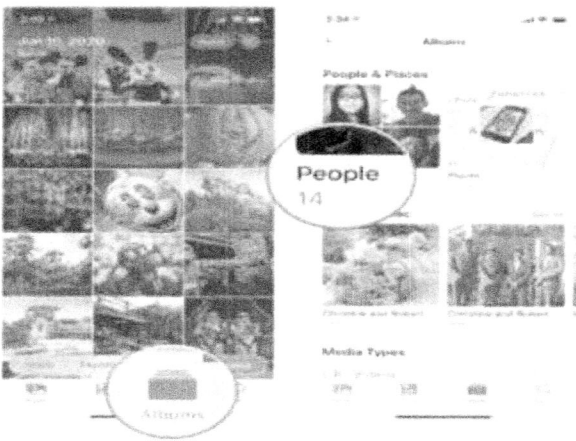

- Click on any **unnamed people** to see images of that person
- From the top, click **Add** name to give them a name
- Click **Next**. Click **Done**

Chapter 14: Music

The music app is great for finding great music and building your playlists.

You can download music, get music from the Apple music service and

Beats 1 radio. Here's how you can make great use of the music function of your device:

Adding songs to music

You have 3 options:

- You can buy music from iTunes store. The songs would automatically be added to your music app. You can also download purchased songs via iCloud if you used another device to buy music.
- You can add music via the Apple music catalog. You do this clicking on the More button next to a track and then clicking Add to my music
- You can also get music by iTunes Sync

Locating Songs in Music
- Click on the **magnifying glass** at top right

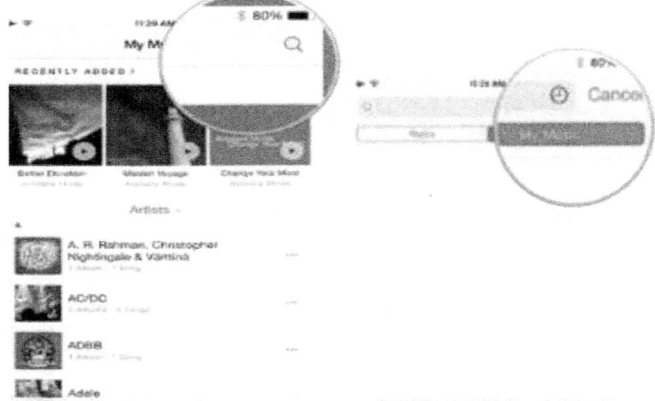

- Next, click on the **My Music** at top right
- Type the song name, artist or album

To Go to Recent Searches to Locate Something:
- Click on the **magnifying glass** at top right
- Click on the **clock** icon at right of the search bar

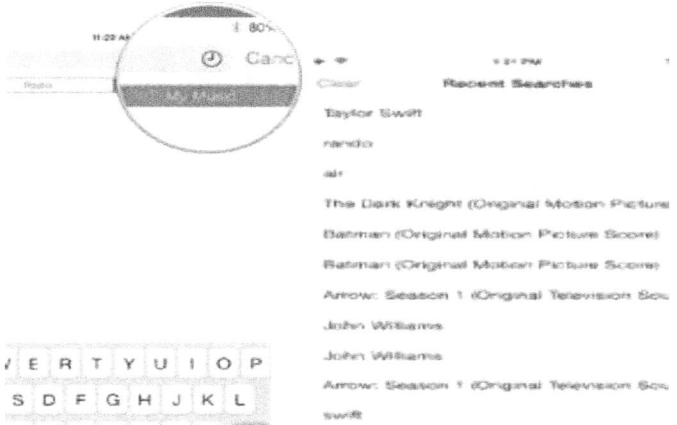

- Click any **recent result** to repeat the search
- Click **Clear** at top left and tap **Clear Recent Searches** to remove the results list

Browsing for Songs in Music
- Click on the **My Music** tab
- Click on the **category** button at the top of the song list

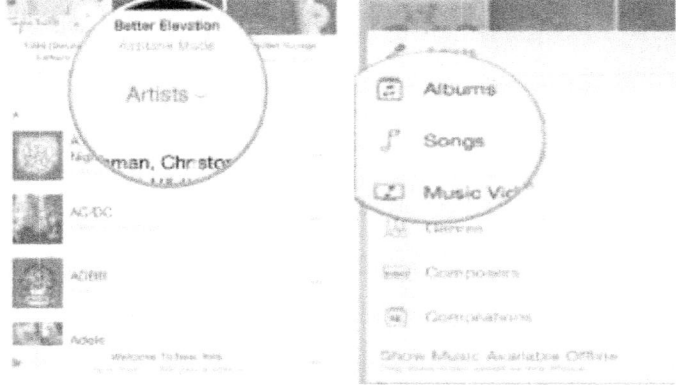

- Click on the category you want to sort either by **Albums, Songs, Music, Videos, Genres, Composers,** or **Compilations**

How to Download Songs

- Click the **More** button that looks like 3 dots to the right of the artist, album, playlist or song

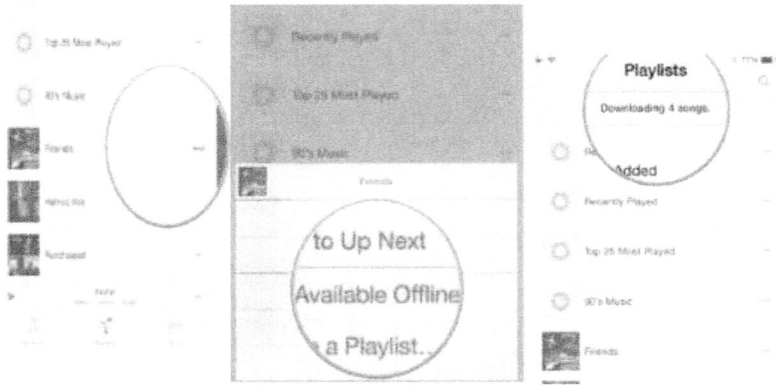

- Click on the **Make Available Offline** button
- Click on the **Downloads** tab to view and organize the caching. When a music is available for offline playback, you would see a small **device icon** at top right of the More button

To Remove Downloaded Songs from Cache

- Click the **More** button to the right of the artist, album, or song you want to expel
- Click the **Remove Download** button
- When the music is removed from the local cache, the **device icon** will not be in evidence at its former place at top right of the More button

Deleting songs from your music library
- Click on the **More** button to the right of the artist, album or song
- Click on **delete**
- Click the **Delete purchase** button

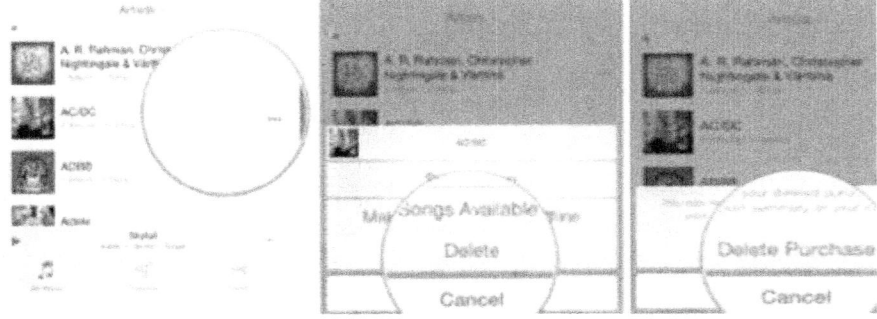

Accessing playlists
- Click the **My Music** tab at bottom right
- Click the **playlist** tab at the top

Playing a playlist
- Click on the **name** of a playlist to play it immediately

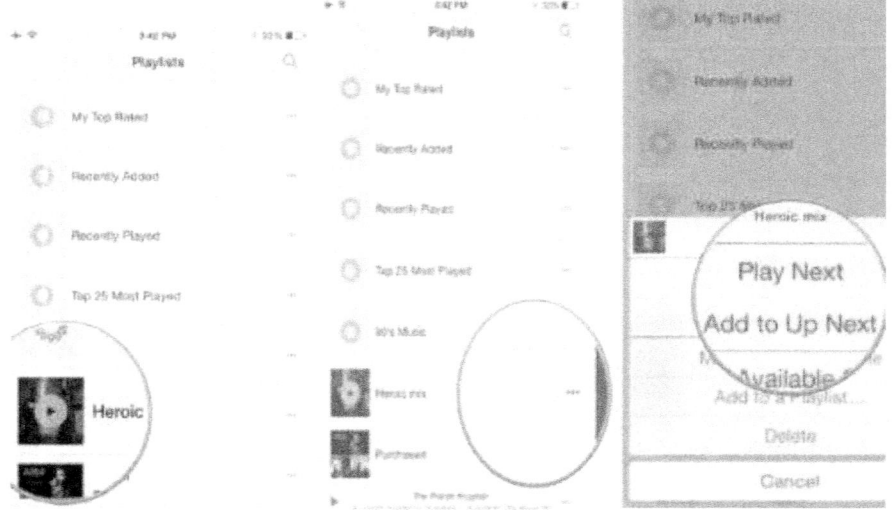

- You can click the **More** button and then click "play Next" to include it to the beginning of your Up Next queue
- You can also click **More** button, then click to **Add to Up Next** to add it to the end of your Up Next queue

Creating a New Playlist
- Click **new**

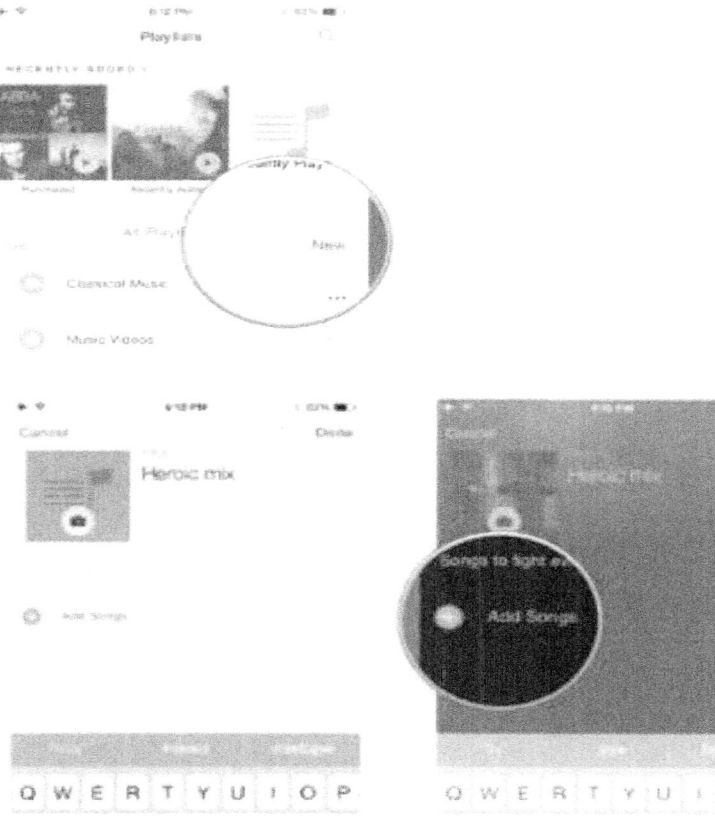

- Type a **title**
- Click the **Camera** icon to select a thumbnail
- Type a **description**
- Click **Add Songs** to begin adding songs
- Click **Done** at top right to end

Adding Tracks to a Playlist
- Click **Edit**
- Click **Add songs**

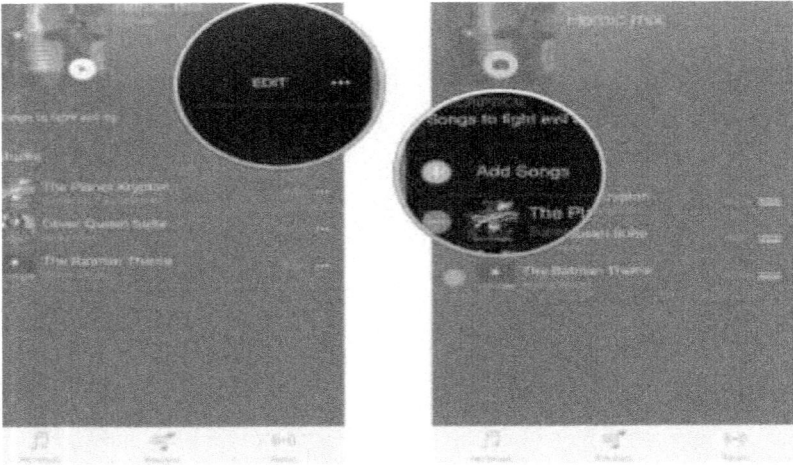

- **Search** out the tracks or songs you want to include
- Click the **+** button to add the track
- Click **Done** at top right to end

In case you want to add tracks from any location in the music app:

- Click on the **More** button to the right of the track you want to add
- Click **Add to playlist**
- Click on the **playlist** you want to add it to

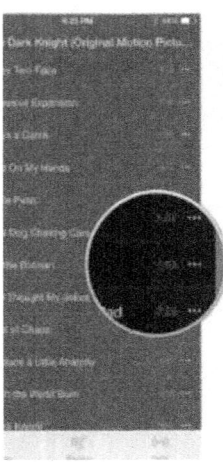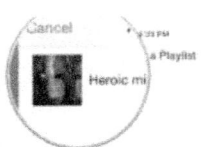

Arranging Tracks on a playlist
- Open the **playlist**
- Click **Edit**

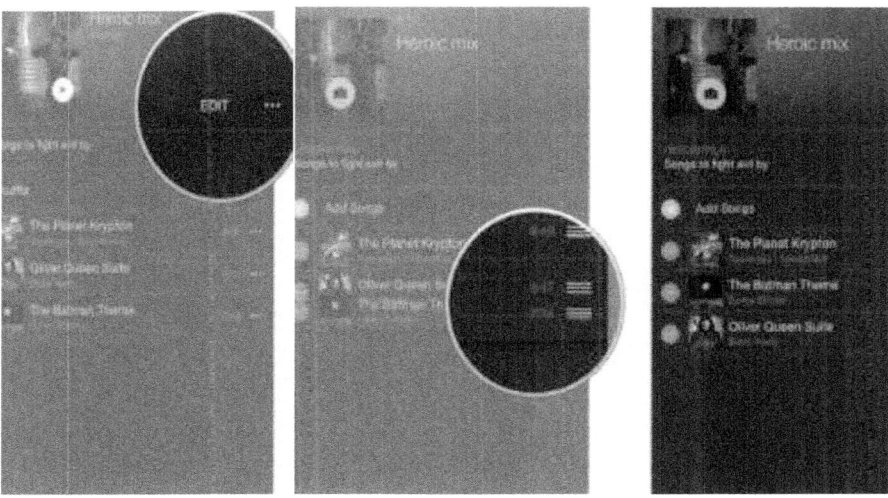

- Tap and hold down on the **grabber** button to the right of the track you want to move
- Drag the **track** to its new position
- Click **Done** at top right to end

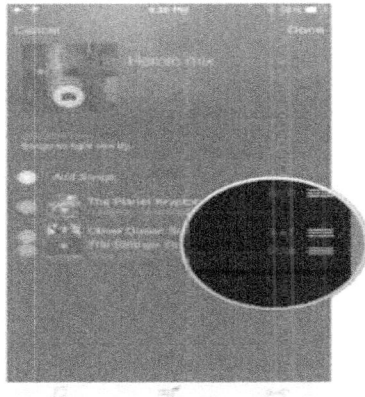 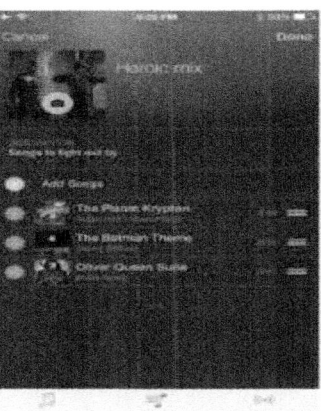

Removing a Track from a Playlist
Locate the **playlist**

- Click on **Edit**. Click the **red –** button to right of the track
- Click the red **Delete** button

 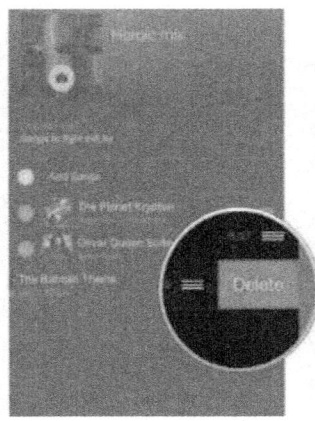 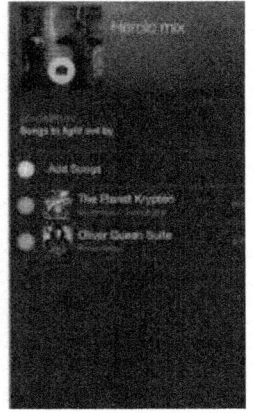

Deleting a playlist
Click on the **More** button to the right of the playlist

Click **Delete**

Click **delete playlist** to confirm

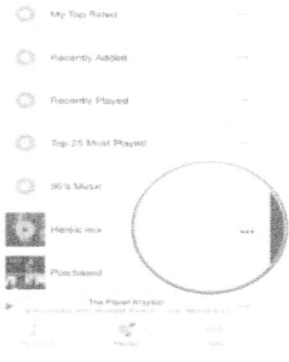 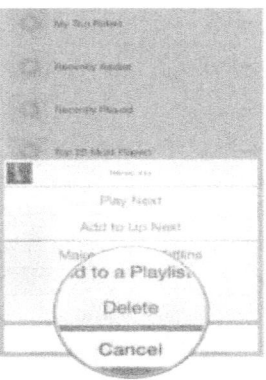 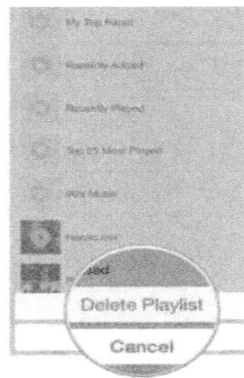

It's possible to delete a playlist from the specific playlist screen itself:

- Click the **More** button
- Click **Delete**

- Click **Delete** playlist to confirm

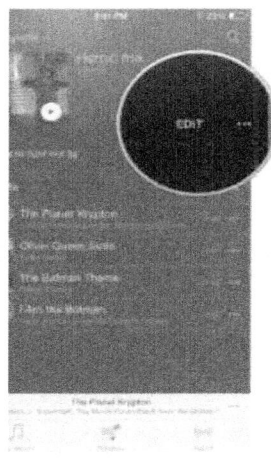  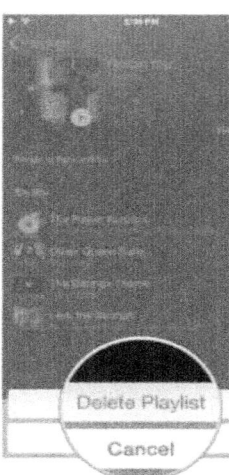

Creating a Genius Playlist

iTunes can do your mixing and matching if you let it. It will accomplish this via the iTunes algorithm. If it's not turned on by default, you can engage it yourself:

- Open **Settings**
- Click on M**usic**

- Switch **Genius** to on and **Accept** the terms and conditions
- Click on the **More** button to the right of a song

- Click on **Create Genius Playlist**

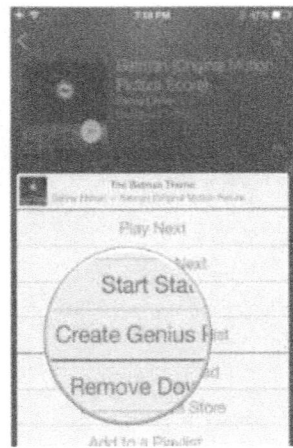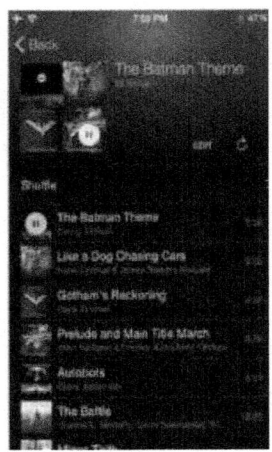

Using Up Next

This is a feature that allows you listen to music you suddenly want to hear without disrupting what you initially had lined up.

Quickly Add Music to up Next from Anywhere
- Locate the **track, album** or **playlist**
- Click the **More** button
- Click on **play Next** to add the music to the front of your Up Next queue or **Add to Up Next** to place it at the end of the queue

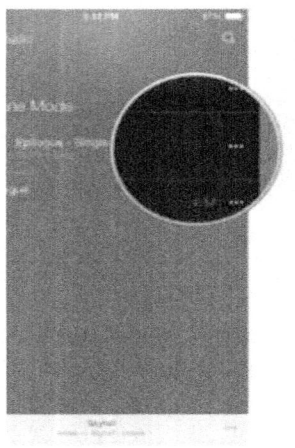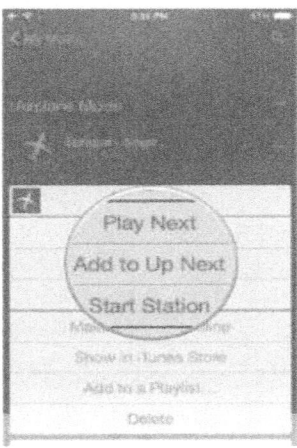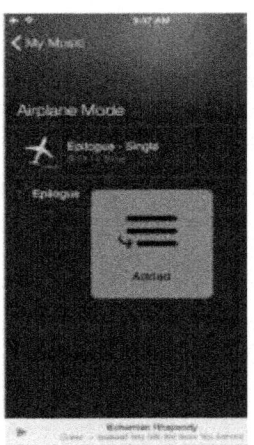

163

How to Quickly clear Up Next from Anywhere
- Locate the **track, album** or **playlist**
- Click on the **track, album** or **playlist** to begin playing it
- Click **Clear Up Next** from the menu

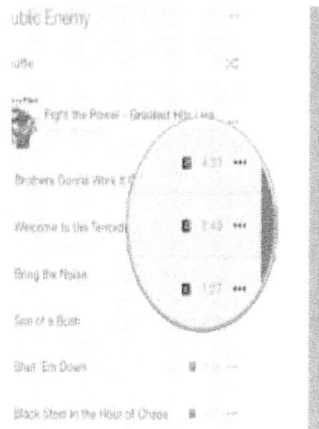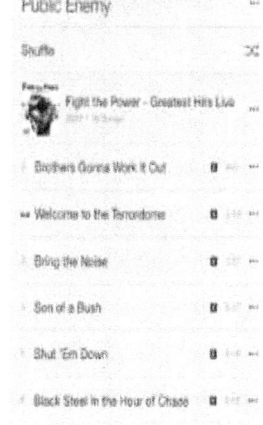

To view Your Up Next Queue
- Find the **mini player** just above the bar
- Click the **track information** button on the mini player to call up the now Playing screen
- Click on the **Up Next** button
- Click the **Done** button

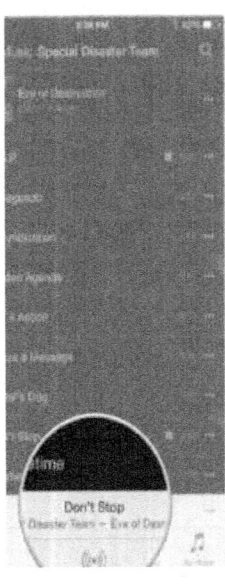  

Viewing Your Up Next History
- From the **Up Next** screen
- Swipe down to show your **Up Next history**
- Click a **track** if you wish to hear it again
- Click **Done**

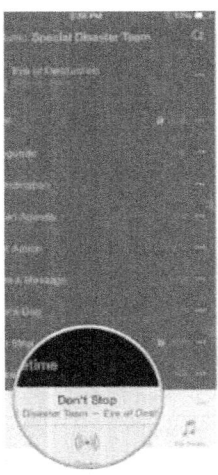  

Adding music to Up Next

- From the **Up Next** screen
- Click on **Add**
- **Search** for the music you wish to include
- Click the+ or the right to add a track, playlist or album

Re-arranging What's Up Next

- From the **Up Next** screen
- Tap and hold the **grabber** button to the right of the track you want to move
- Move the track to the desired position

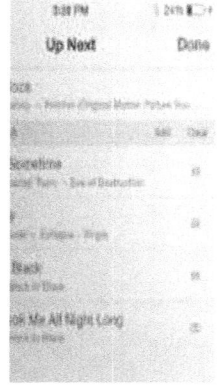 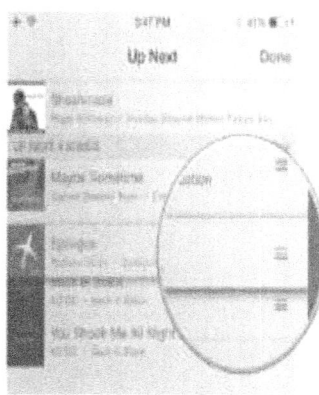 

Removing a Track from Up Next
- From the **Up Next** screen
- Swipe to the left on the **track** to show the red Remove button
- Click the red **Remove** button

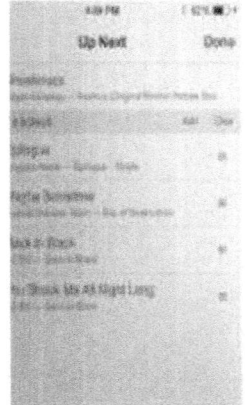 

Clearing Music from Up Next
- Open the **Up Next** screen
- Click on **clear** at the top
- Click **Up Next** at the bottom to confirm.

Chapter 15: Mail

Setting Up Mail on Your Device

- Open **Settings**
- Click **Accounts & Passwords**
- Click **Add Account**

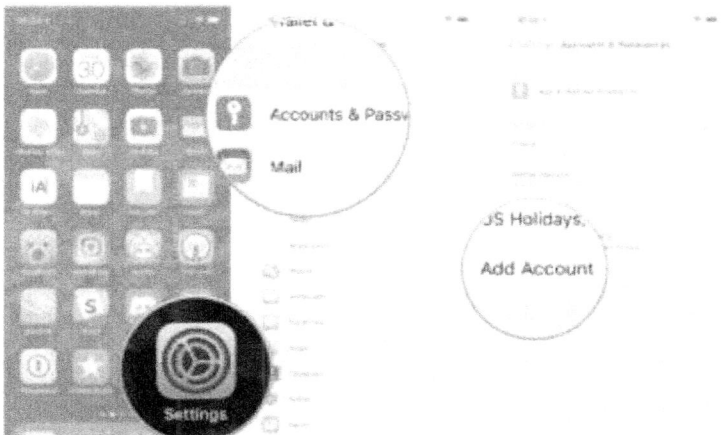

- Click **Google**
- Click **continue** if asked to confirm that you want to allow Google.com to sign in on your device
- Type your **Google account** details

- Ensure that the **toggles** for mail, contacts and calendars are in the "on" or "off" positions depending on the settings you want

168

- Click **Save**

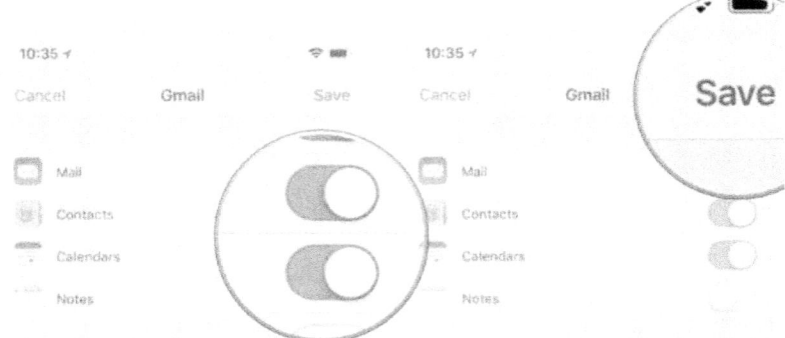

Setting Up Outlook.com Mail
- Repeat step 1-3 as above (setting up mail)
- Click **Outlook.com**
- Type your **Outlook.com account details**

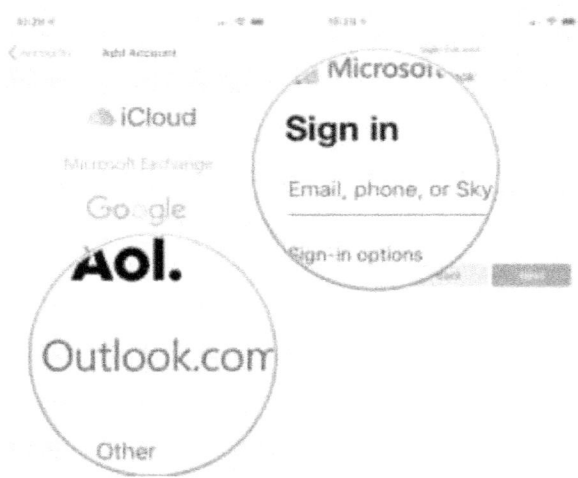

- Repeat steps 9 and 10 above (setting up mail)

Setting up Exchange Mail
- Repeat steps 1-3 as above
- Click **Exchange**
- Type your **Exchange email address**

- Click **Next**

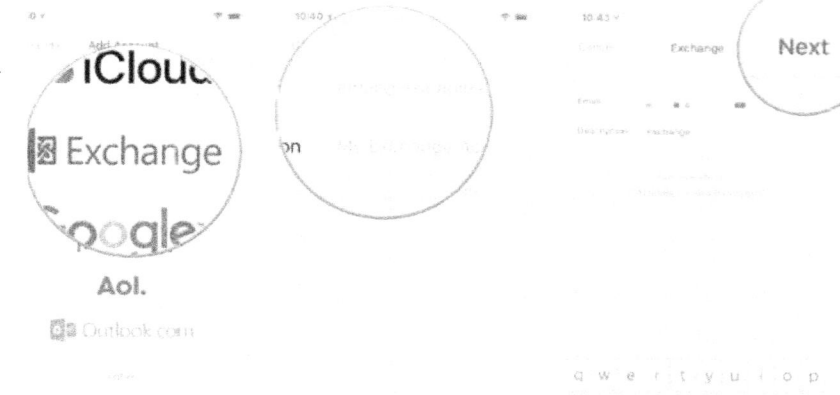

- Click **Configure Manually**
- Type your **Exchange account information** if you chose to configure your account manually
- Click **Next**

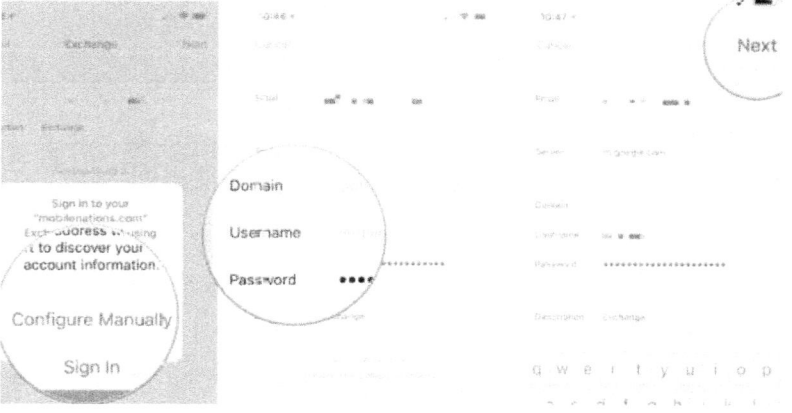

- Repeat step 9 and 10 above

Setting Up IMAP/POP, CalDav and CardDAV
- Follow steps 1-3 as above
- Click **Other**

- Choose the **type** of account you want to configure. Choose mail for an email account CalDAV for a calendar and CardDAV for contacts

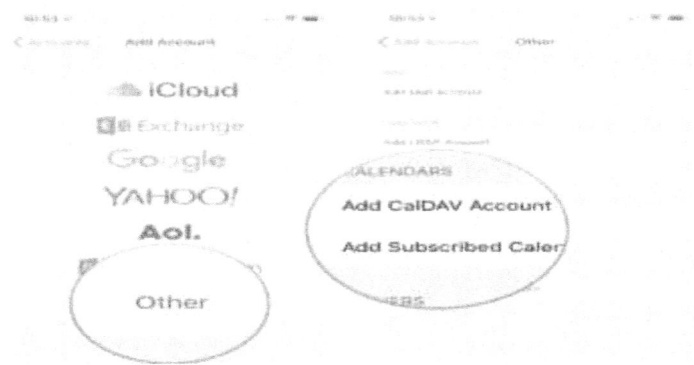

- Type your **account information**
- Click **Next**
- Click **Done**

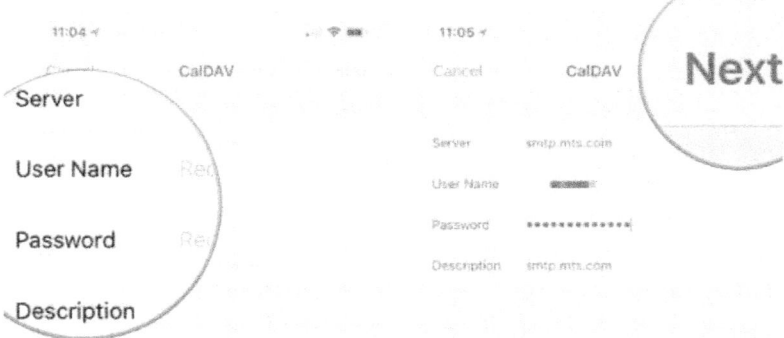

Setting Up a Default Email
- Open **Settings**
- Click **Mail**
- Navigate down and click **Default Account**
- Click the **account** you would like to use as default

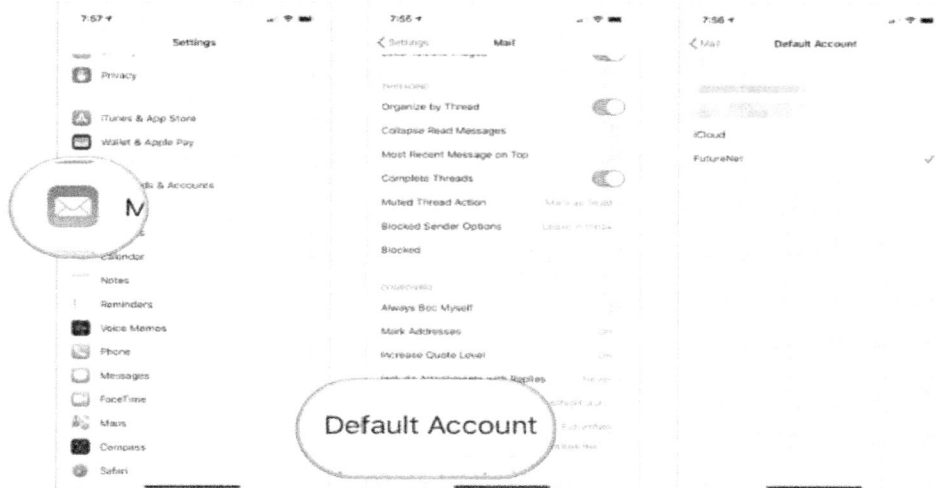

Switching Between Email Accounts
- Open **Mail**
- Click the **Compose** button
- Click the **From field**
- Click the **account** from the picker that you would like to use and the mail will be sent from the selected account

Disabling an Email Account

- Open **Settings**
- Click **Passwords & Accounts**
- Click the **account** you want to disable
- Switch **Mail** off

 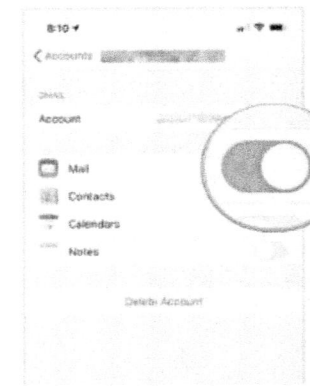

Deleting an Email Account

- Open **Settings**
- Click **Passwords & accounts**
- Click the **account** you want to delete
- Click **Delete Account**

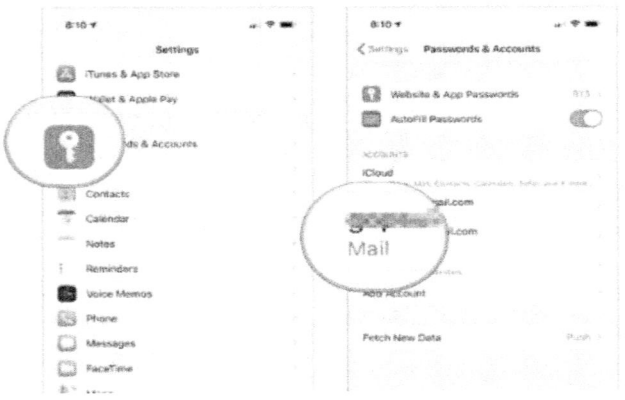 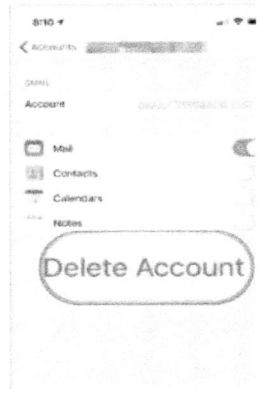

Getting New Mail Notifications
- Open **Settings**
- Click on **Notifications** and navigate up until you get to mail
- Click on **Mail**
- Click on the **switch** beside **Allow Notifications**

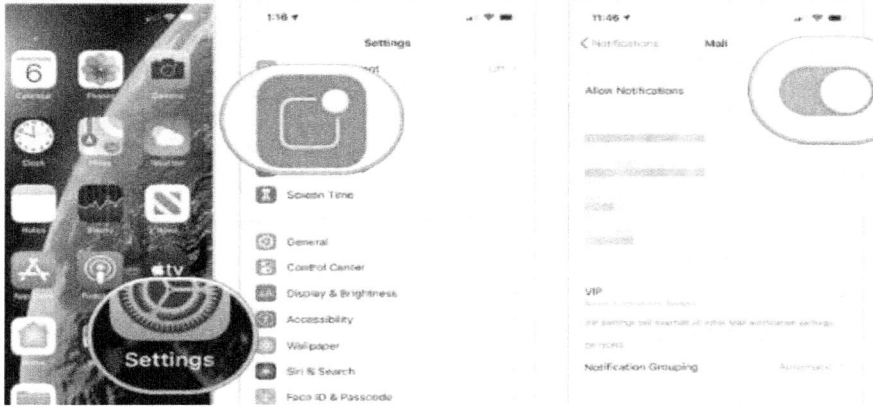

- Click on the **mail** you wish to adjust its notification settings

You can decide to adjust and customize your notifications to add sounds, notifications in the notifications center, badge app icons, etc.

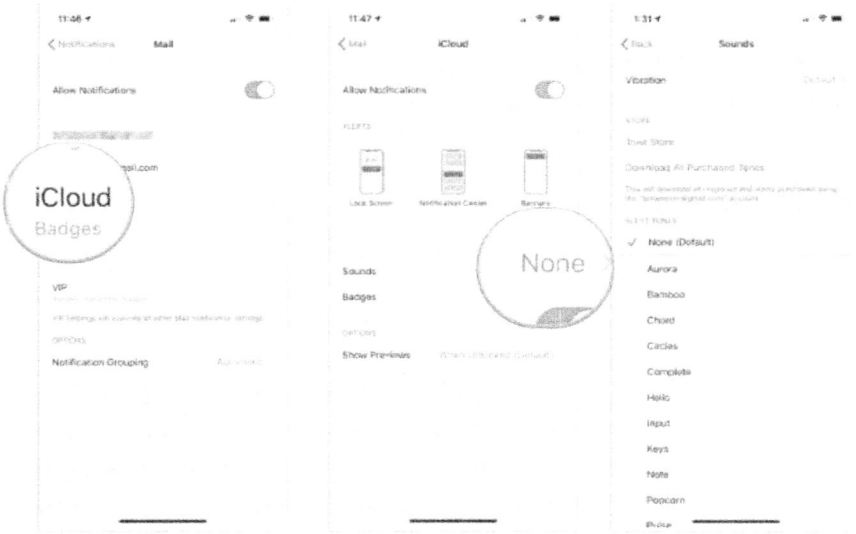

Managing Small Accounts
- Open **Settings**
- Navigate to **Passwords & Accounts**
- Click the **account** you would like to manage and adjust your email account

Changing Preview Lines
- Go to **Settings**
- Click **Mail**
- Select **Preview** and select the number of lines to alter the mail preview display

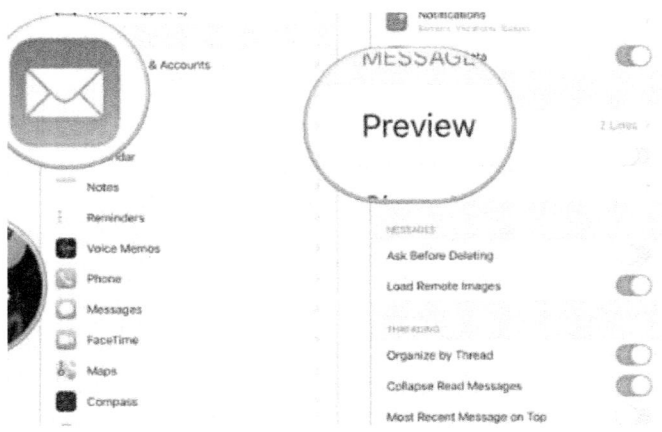

Displaying To/Cc Labels
- Go to **Settings**
- Click **Mail**
- Click the **switch** next to Show To/Cc Labels so it would change to a green color

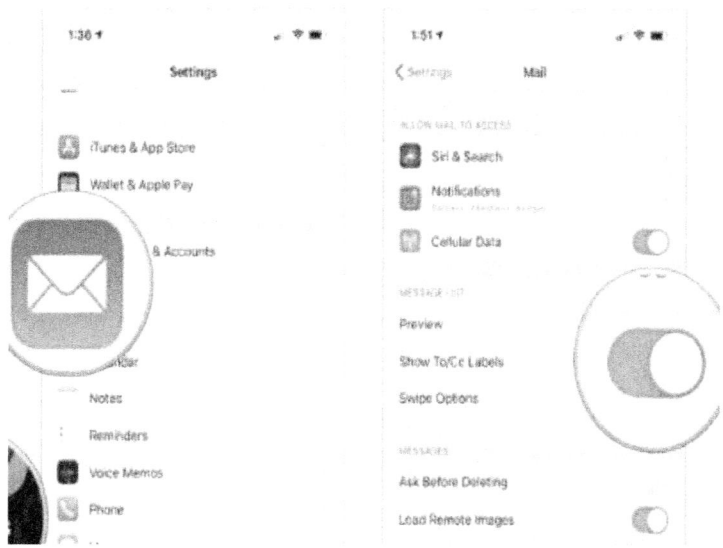

Adjusting Swipe Options
- Open **Settings**
- Click **Mail**
- Click **Swipe Options**

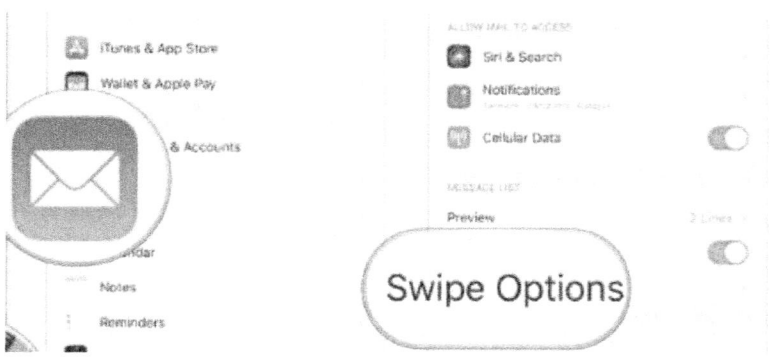

- Click **Swipe Left** or **Swipe Right** to change the slide options
- Click **flag** or **Move Message** to set the slide direction

How to toggle Ask Before Deleting
- Open the **Settings** app
- Click **Mail**
- Click the **switch** next to **Ask Before Deleting** so it would become green

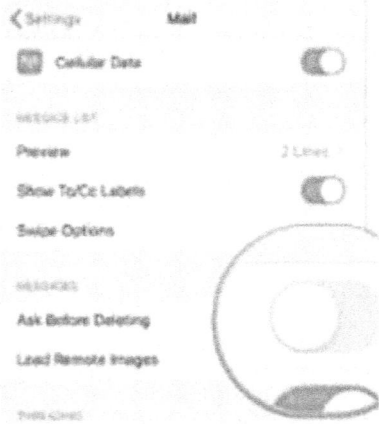

Loading Remote Images
- Open **Settings**
- Click **Mail**

- Click the **switch** next to **Load Remote Images**

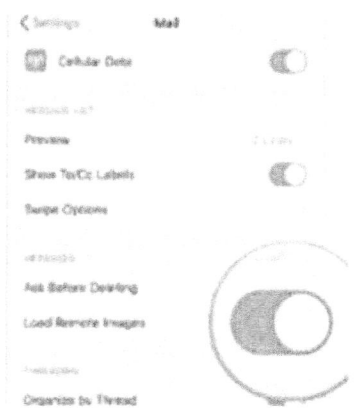

Organizing Emails by Thread
- Open **settings**
- Click **mail**
- Click on the **switch** next to **Organize by Thread**

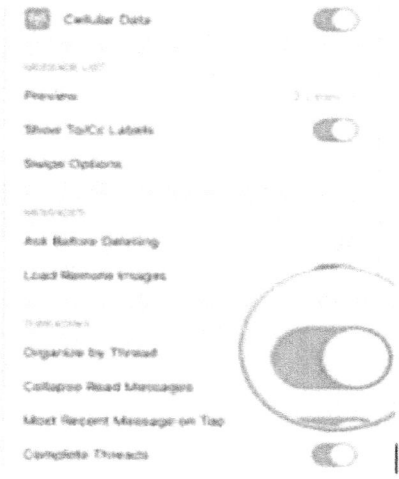

Collapsing Read Messages
- Open **Settings**

- Click **Mail**
- Click the **switch** next to **collapse Read Massages**

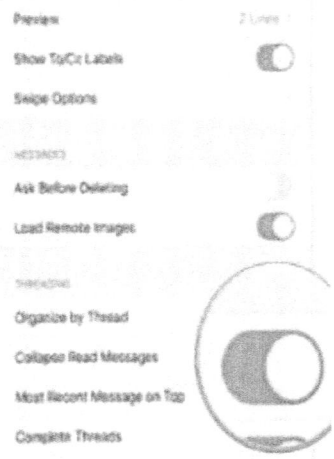

Moving a Thread's Most Recent Message to the Top
- Open **Settings**
- Click **Mail**
- Click the **switch** next to **Most recent Message in Top**

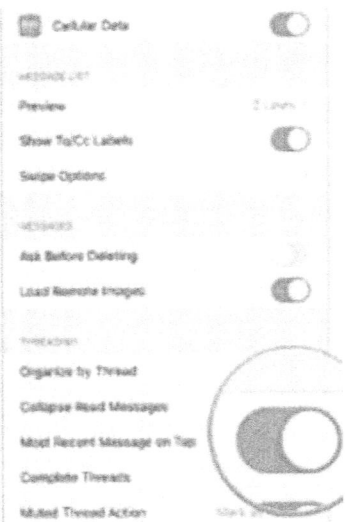

Turning Complete Threads on and Off

- Open **Settings**
- Click **Mail**
- Click the switch next to **Complete Threads**

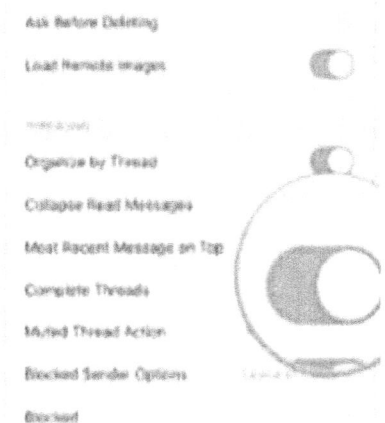

How to Turn Always Bcc Myself on and off

- Open **Settings**
- Click **Mail**
- Click the **switch** next to **Always Bcc Myself**

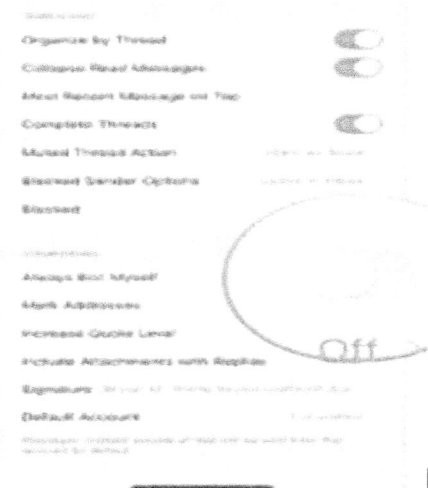

Marking Addresses

- Open **Settings**
- Click **Mail**
- Click **Mark Addresses**
- Enter the **type of address** you would like to mark

Turning Increase Quote Level on and off

- Open **Settings**. Click **Mail**. Click **Increase Quote level**
- Click the **switch** next to **Increase Quote Level**

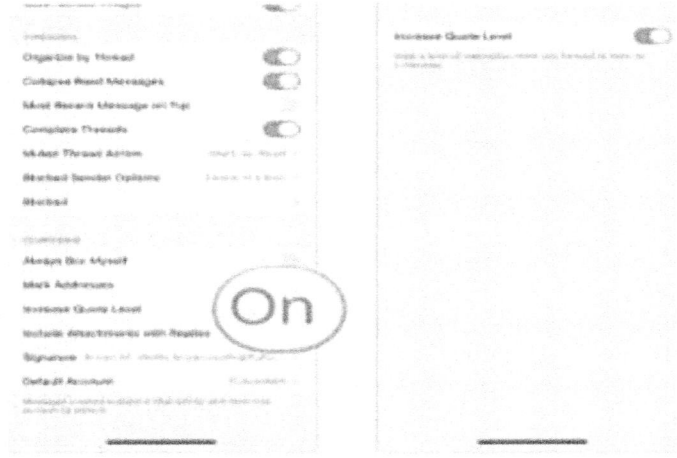

Setting Your Signature
- Open **Settings**
- Click **Mail**
- Click **Signature**
- Add your **new signature**

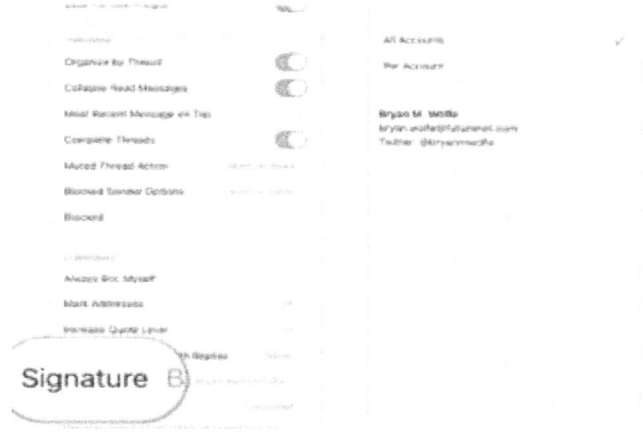

Mark an Email as Read or Unread
- Open the **Mail app**
- Click **Edit** at upper right

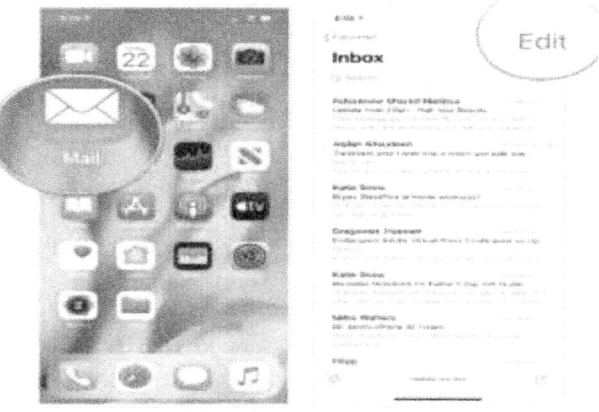

- Select any **mail** you would like to mark as read
- Click **Mark** at lower left corner

- Click **Mark as Read** and if the messages you selected have been read, you can click **Mark as Unread**

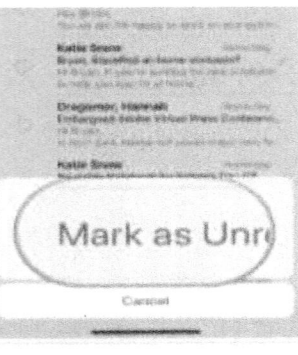

Flagging an Email
- Open the **Mail app**
- Click **Edit** at upper right
- Select the **message** you like to flag
- Click **Mark** at lower left of your screen
- Click **Flag** and if the message you selected was already flagged, you can click **Unflag**

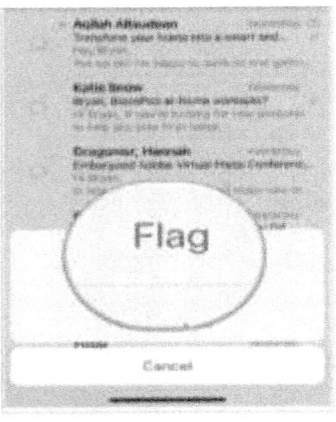

183

Adding New Mailboxes

- Open the **Mail** app
- Click **Edit** at upper right
- Select **New Mailbox** at lower right corner

- Enter a name for your mailbox in the **Name** field
- Click the **Mailbox Location** field to attach your new folder to an account
- Select a **main mailbox** in which you would like to locate your new mailbox

Moving Messages to Different Mailboxes

- Open the **Mail app**
- Select the **mailbox** where the message you want to move is located
- Click **Edit**

- Choose the **message** you want to move
- Select **Move**
- Choose the **mailbox** to which you would like to move the message

Adding Contacts to Your VIP List
- Open **Mail app**
- Select the **VIP** under your normal inbox
- Click **Add VIP**

- Select a person from your contacts list to add to the VIP list
- You can still select Add VIP to add more

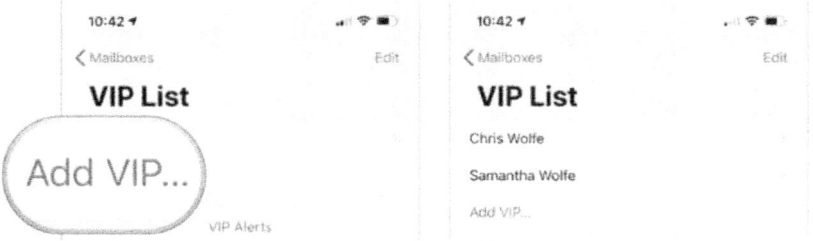

Filtering Inboxes in the Mail App
- Open the **mail app**
- From **Mailboxes,** select your mail account
- Click an **inbox**

- Select the **filter** button at left corner of the screen
- Click **Filtered By**
- Choose the **category** to be filtered
- Click **Done** at upper right part of the screen

Unsubscribing to Mailing Lists
- Open the **Mail app**
- Choose an **email** from a mailing list that you don't want to receive anymore
- Click **Unsubscribe** at the top of the mail
- Select **Unsubscribe** when asked to confirm

Creating a New Email in the Mail App

- Open the **Mail app**
- Click the **Compose** button
- Enter the **recipient email address** or name of the person that the mail is intended for

- Select the **subject field** and add the subject of the mail
- Click the **message field** and type the message
- When you are done, click **Send** at top right corner

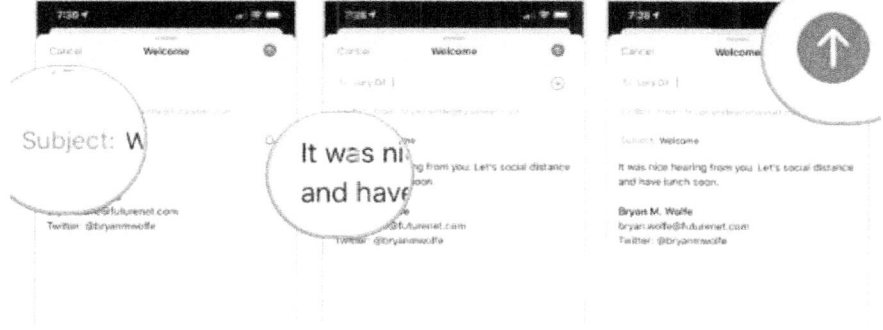

Choosing an Email Address from Your Contacts in the Mail App

- Open the **Mail app**
- Click the **Compose** button at bottom right corner of screen

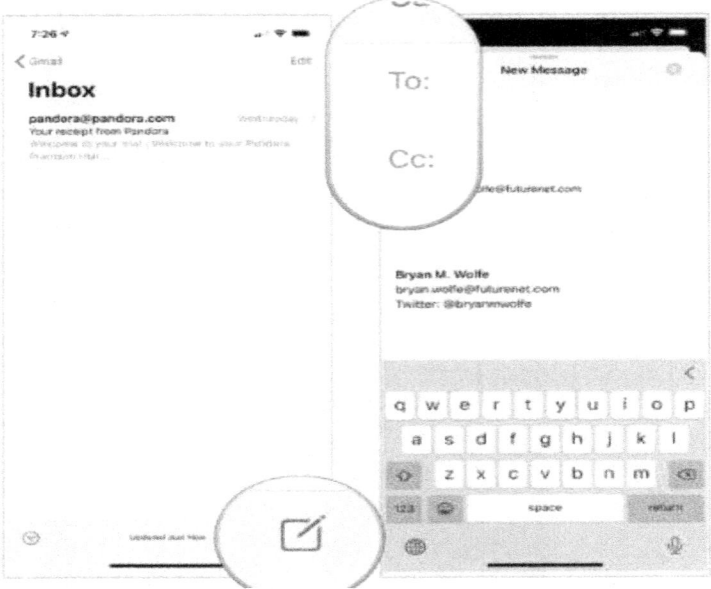

- Select the + sign in the circle ** to call up your contacts
- Choose the **contact** you would like to add and they would be automatically included to the mail

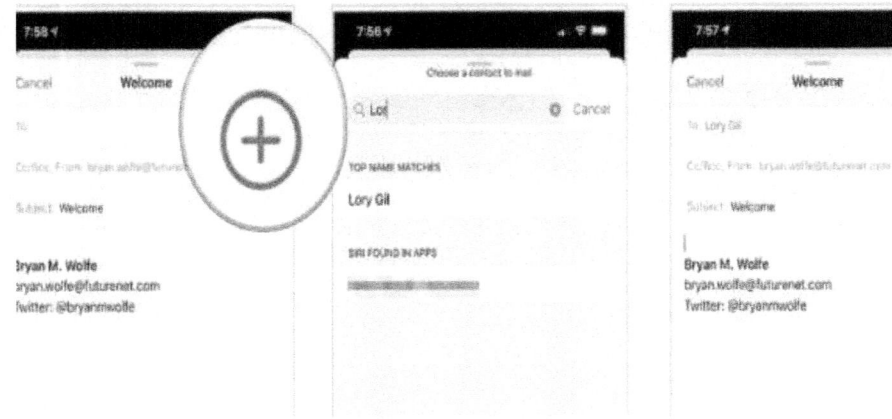

189

How to Access Drafts in the Mail App
- Open the **Mail** app
- Click on and hold the **Compose** button at lower right corner and the drafted emails would be brought up
- Select the **email draft** you want to edit and send when you are done

Using Siri to Send Email
- Push and hold the home button or say" **Hey Siri"** to engage the feature
- Next you can say **"send an email to John"**
- If siri presents you with more than one option, you will have to click on the correct one or you could give the command with specifics that would enable siri to identify the correct recipient
- Next, let Siri know the **email subject**

- Let Siri know the **email content**
- Allow Siri to **confirm the email content**
- Click **Send** or say **Yes** to send the email. If you have issues with the mail, you can either tell Siri to change any aspect of it or cancel it entirely

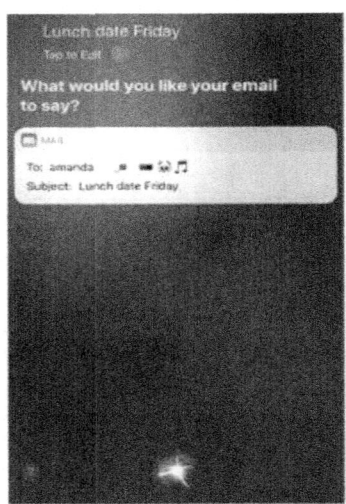
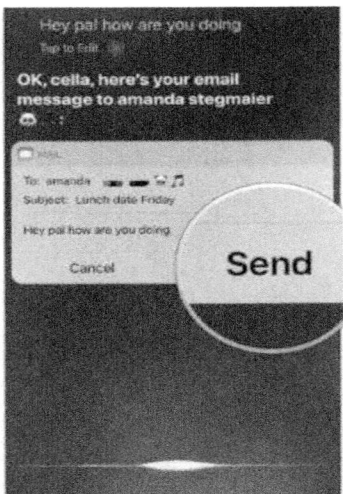

Making Siri Read Your Unread Emails
- Push and hold the Home button or say **Hey Siri** to activate it
- Next, ask it to **"Read my unread emails"**
- Click on any email to see it in the app

Asking Siri to Respond to an Email

- Open the **Mail app**
- Click on **inbox**
- Click on the **mail** you want to respond to

- Push and hold the **Home button** or say **"Hey Siri"** to activate it
- Next, ask Siri to **"Respond to this mail"**
- Let siri know what you want the **email to say**

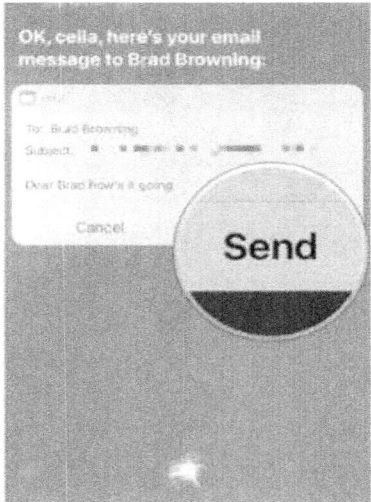

Using Siri to Create a Contact Relationship

- To be able to do this, you will have to let siri know your relationships so the voice assistant would be able to serve you well. You have to let siri know who your wife or husband is, boss, best friend, children etc. you have two ways. You could either edit the information or tell siri verbally
- Push and hold the **Home button** or say **"Hey Siri"** to wake the voice assistant up
- Let siri know the relationship making sure to say the name as you saved it in your contacts. For e.g. **john smith is my boss**
- Respond with **Yes** or click **Yes** when Siri seeks a confirmation. The voice assistant will also let you know that the relationship has been added

Adding a New Email Address to a Contact in the Mail App
- Launch the **Mail app**

- Click the **email** with the new contact
- Click the **email address**

- Click **Add to existing contacts** and choose a contact
- You can equally click **Update contact** if it's labeled under the correct name
- Click **Update** at upper right corner of screen

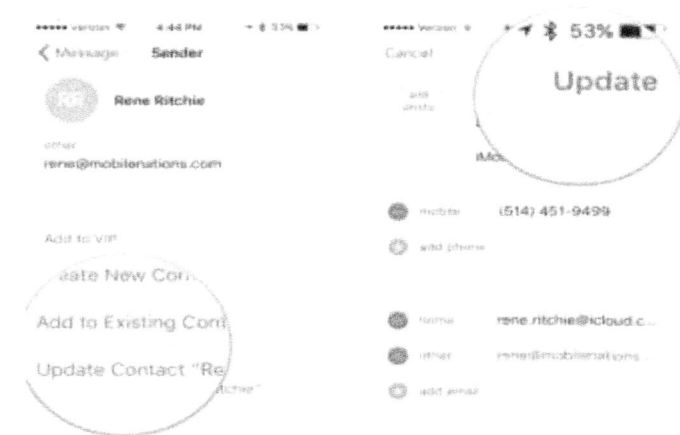

Inserting a Photo or Video into an Email in the Mail App
- Open the **Mail app**
- Click on **Compose** button at bottom right corner

- Enter the **sender info, subject, and body fields** just as you would for a regular email

- Click in **body** and a menu will appear
- Select the **photo icon**
- Choose the **photo** or **video** you would like to insert
- Click the **send** button at upper right corner when you are done composing the mail

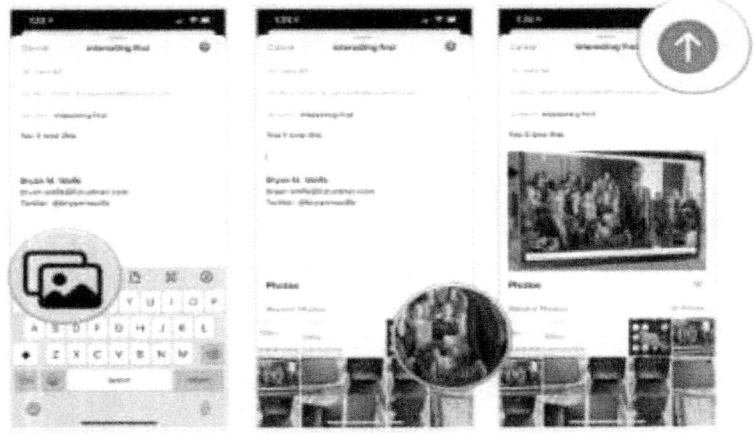

Adding an Attachment to a Mail
- Open the **Mail app**
- Click on the **Compose** button at bottom right
- Enter the **sender info, subject and body** fields like a regular email
- Click in the **body** and a menu will appear
- Select the **Attachment icon**
- Choose the **file** you want to send
- Click **send** at upper right when you are done composing the email

Saving a Mail as PDF in Mail
- Launch the **Mail app**
- Click an **email** you want to save as PDF
- Select the **action** button

- Navigate down and click **Print** to open the printer options
- Pinch open the **thumbnail** of the first page of your email

- Click the **Share** button at upper right corner of screen
- Choose the **app** you want to save or share your PDF converted email to

Chapter 16: Contacts

Adding a Contact to Your Device
- Open the **Contacts** app
- Click on the + sign at top right corner
- From the top section, you can enter all the necessary information like
- Contact's first name. Contact's last name. Contact's company

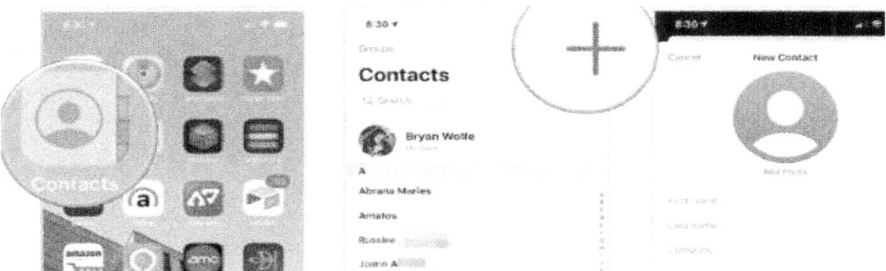

- Click on the **green + symbol** next to add phone number
- Key in the contact's **phone number**
- Click on **Done** at top right to save the contact

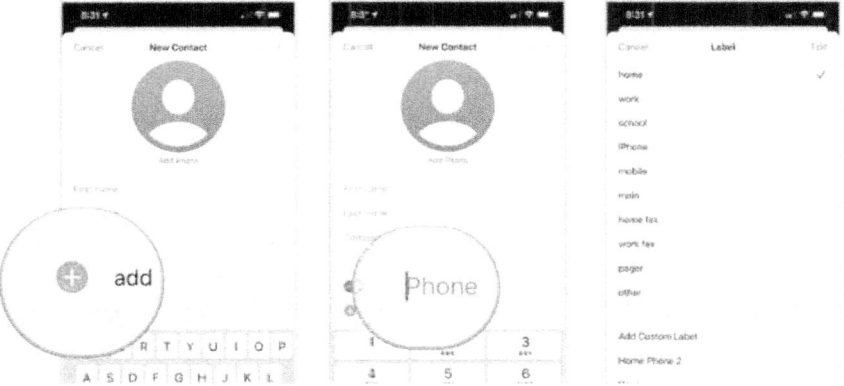

Updating an Existing Contact
- Open the **Contacts** app
- Click on the **contact** you want to update

- Click on the **Edit** button at top right corner
- You can now add any other information such as phone numbers, email address etc

Finding an Existing Contact
- Open the **Contacts** app
- Click on the **search bar**
- Enter the **contact's name** to find them

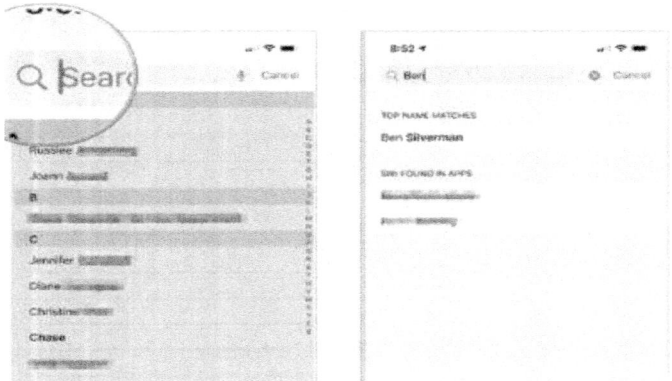

If it just so happens that you can't remember a contact's name but you are sure it's in your contact, you can find it by the first letter in their name.

- Open the **Contacts** app
- Click on a **letter** at right side of your screen

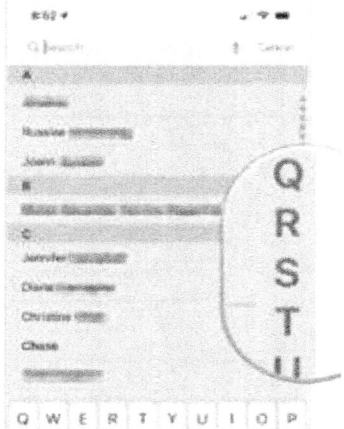

Sharing a Contact
- Go to the **Contacts** app
- Click on the **contact** you want to share
- Click on **Share Contact**

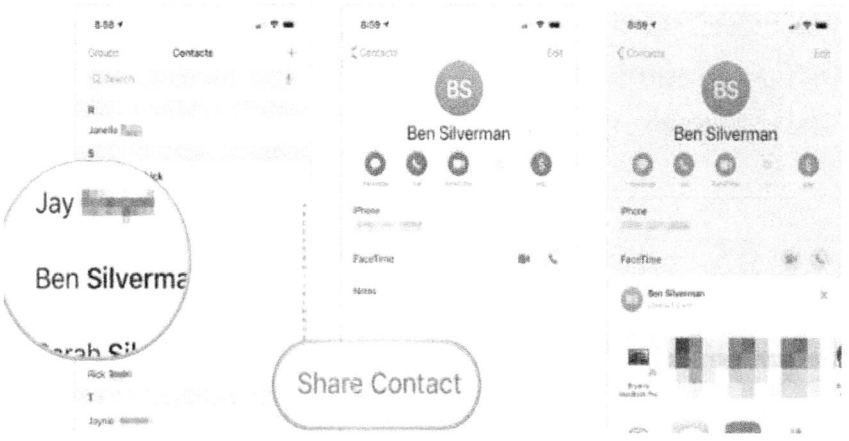

There are different ways to share the contact and you will have to use the one best suited for your intentions and follow the directions to send.

Assigning Photos to Contacts
- Open the **photos app**
- Click the **photo** you want to assign to a contact
- Click the **Share** button at bottom left of your screen
- Click on **Assign to Contact**

- Click on the **contact** you want to assign the photo to
- Next, drag and pinch the **photo** to scale and set it as you like
- Click **choose** at bottom right of screen
- Click **update** at top right of screen

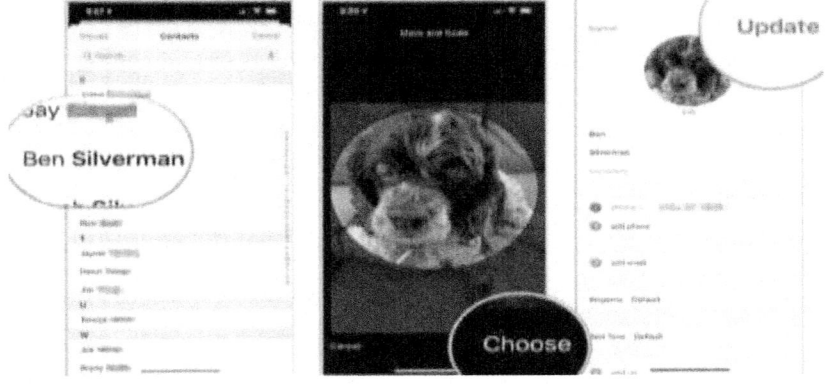

Deleting a Contact
- Open the **Contacts** app
- Click on the **contact** you want to delete
- Click **Edit** at top right corner

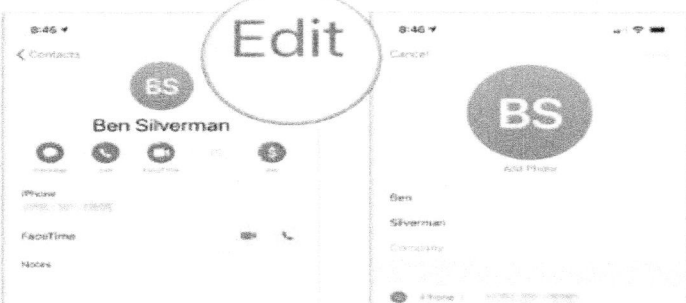

- Navigate down to the **bottom of the page**
- Click on **Delete contact**
- Repeat step 6 again

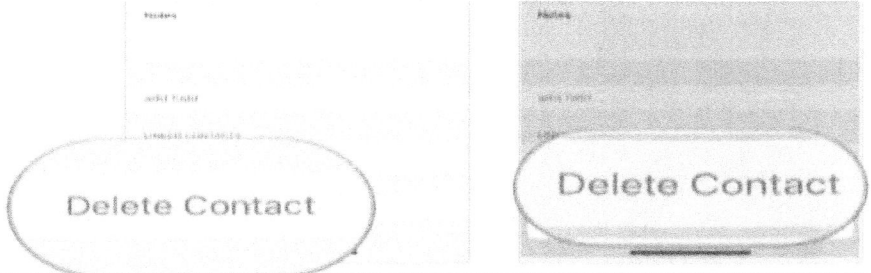

Chapter 17: Calendar

With calendar, it's easier to organize your appointments, share agendas, invite family, friends and colleagues to events and never forget important the important stuff. Calendar is compatible with iCloud, Google calendar, Microsoft Outlook etc.

Set up

Everyone has an existing email account with contact and calendar for organizing their daily appointments. All you need do is sign in to your account and open mail, calendar or contacts on your device and everything is automatically synced.

Changing the Default Time Zone for Calendar Alerts

- Open **Settings**
- Click **Calendar**

- Click **Time zone override**
- Turn on the **Time Zone Override** switch
- Click **Time zone**

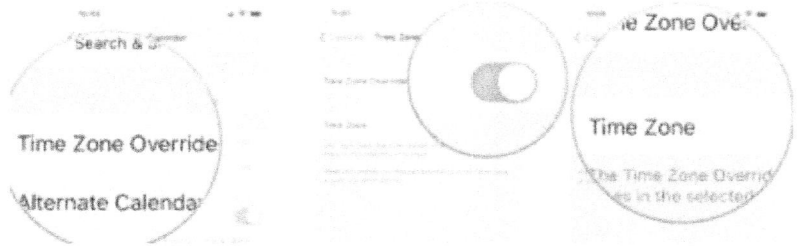

- Find the **city** you want to change the time zone to
- Click the **city** to change the default time zone for your calendar app

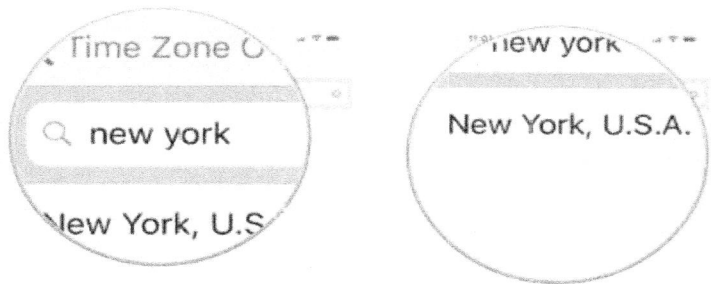

Selecting an Alternate Calendar
- Open **Settings**
- Click **Calendar**
- Click **Alternate Calendars**
- Choose between **Chinese, Hebrew or Islamic**

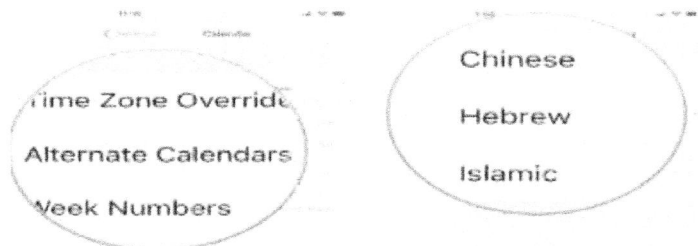

Managing Calendar Syncing
- Open the **Settings app**
- Click **Calendar**

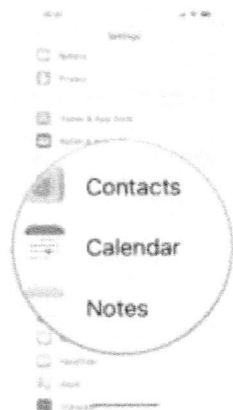

- Click **Sync**
- Select the **time frame** you want to sync back to

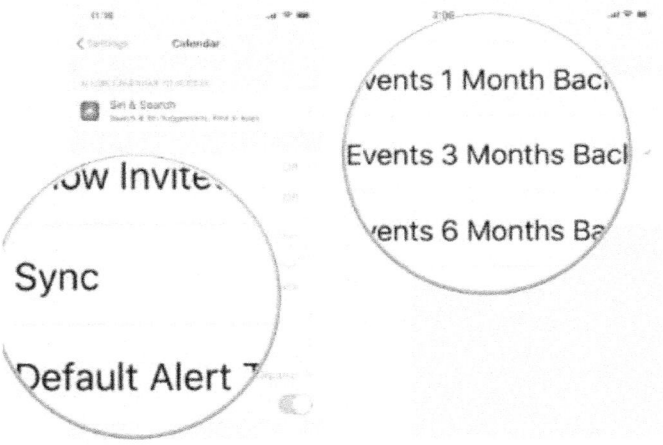

Setting Default Alert Times
- Open the **settings app**
- Click **calendar**
- Click **Default Alert Times**

205

- Choose the **alert** you want to set a default time for
- Specify the **time** you want to get the alert

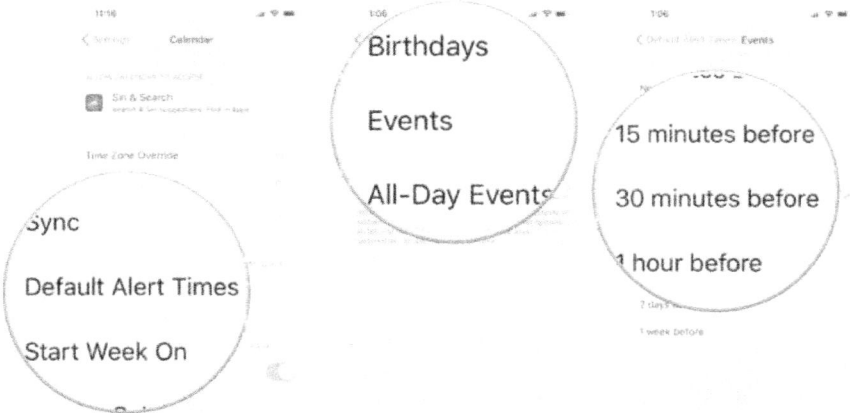

Setting a Reminder to Leave on Time
- Open **settings**
- Click **Calendar**
- Click **Default Alert Times**
- Switch **the Time to Leave** button on

Setting the start of Your Week
- Open **Settings**
- Click **Calendar**
- Click **Start Week On**

- Click a **day of the week**

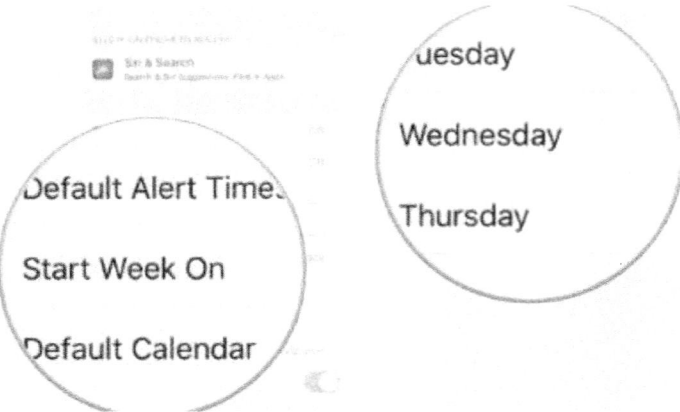

Setting a Default Calendar
- Open **Settings**
- Click **Calendar**
- Click **default calendar**
- Choose the **calendar** you want to be the default

How to turn events in Apps on and off
- Open **Settings**
- Click **Calendar**
- Click **Siri & Search**

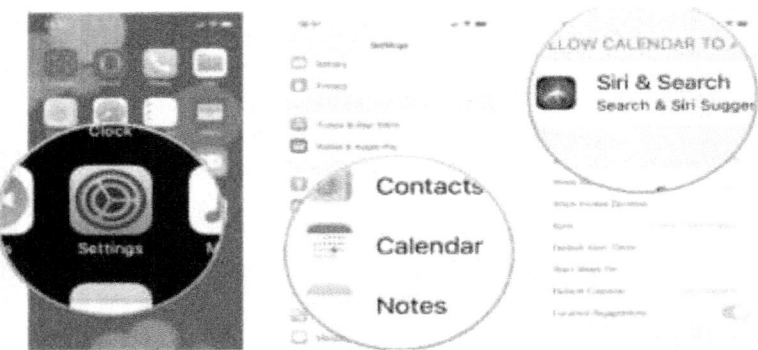

- Next, turn **Search & Siri Suggestions** on or off

- Switch **Find Events in Other Apps** on or off based on your preferences

Creating a Calendar Event
- Open the **Calendar** app
- Click the + symbol at upper right-hand corner
- Type a **title, date** and **time** to your event

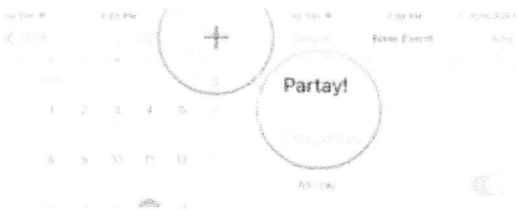

- Decide if you want the event to be an **all-day event.** If the event is time bound, you can turn the option off
- You can customize the calendar event in case it holds often.
- Click **Repeat**
- Select **how frequently** your event will repeat

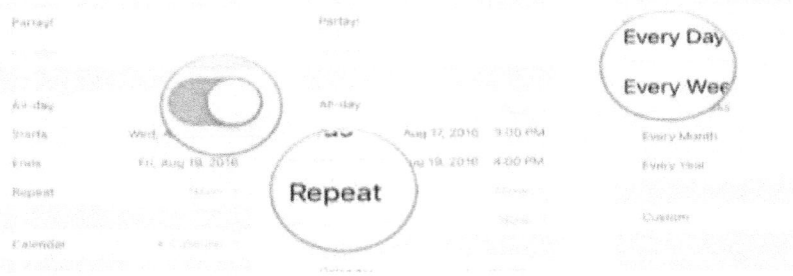

- Select an alert if you want to be notified of an event
- Click **Alert**
- Specify when you want to be alerted

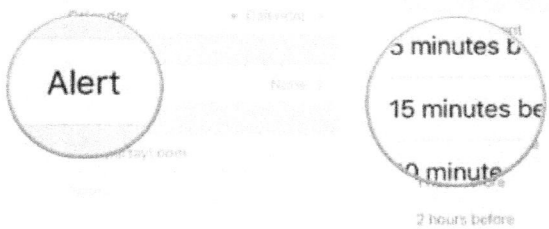

- Type a **URL** if there is a website associated with your event
- Click **Add** at upper right-hand corner to save your entry

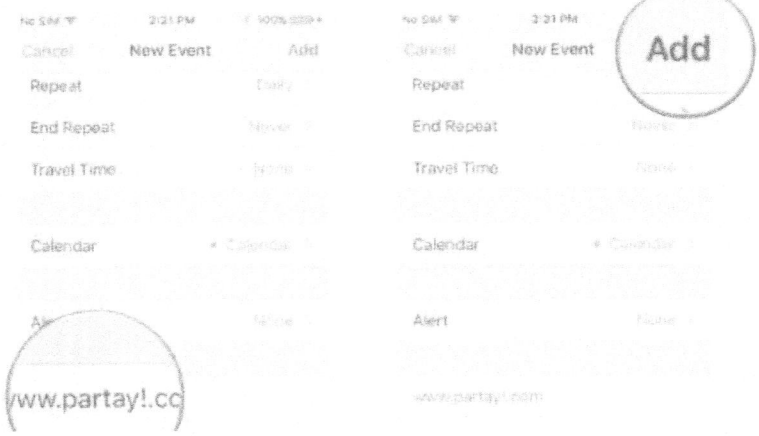

Editing a Calendar Event
- Open the **Calendar** app

209

- Click the **day** on which your event takes place
- Click on the **event** you want to edit
- Click on **Edit** at upper right-hand corner
- You can now change anything you want to and click **Done** when you are through

Deleting a Calendar Event
- Open the **Calendar** app
- Click on the **month** or **day** the event is to hold
- Click the **event** you want to delete
- Click on **Delete Event** at the bottom of the screen
- Click **Delete Event** again to confirm. If it's a repeating event, you want to choose to **Delete This Event Only** or **Delete All Future Events**

Moving a Calendar Event or Appointment by Dragging and Dropping

- Open the **Calendar** app
- Switch the list view to **off** if it's not already
- Click on the specific **day** you need to move things around for
- Click and hold on the **event** you need to change the time for.
- Next, drag the **event** to the time you need to move it to and **release it** when it's at the correct time

Sharing an Event

- Open the **Calendar** app
- You have the option of **creating a new event** or **click on an existing event** you want to share
- Click on the **Edit** button

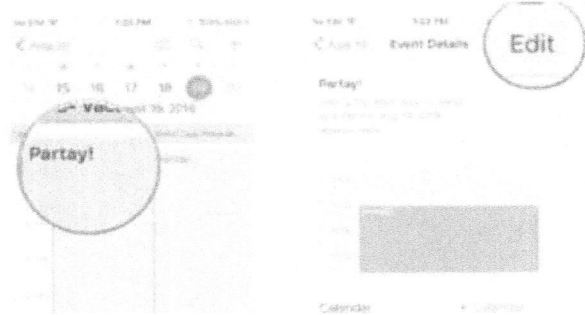

- Click on **Invitees**

- Next, **Add** all the email addresses of the recipients
- You have to do this for anyone you want to invite
- Click **Done** at upper right

Creating a Calendar Event with Siri
- Engage siri via holding down the **Home or Power button** or you can say **"Hey Siri"**
- Let siri know what you want to schedule along with details like day or date, event, and time
- Siri would now display a preview of your event and ask for your confirmation
- Should you not be satisfied with the event details, you can ask siri to **Change** to edit the information
- If you change your mind, you can **cancel**
- If you want it included to your calendar, reply with a **Yes** when siri needs a confirmation

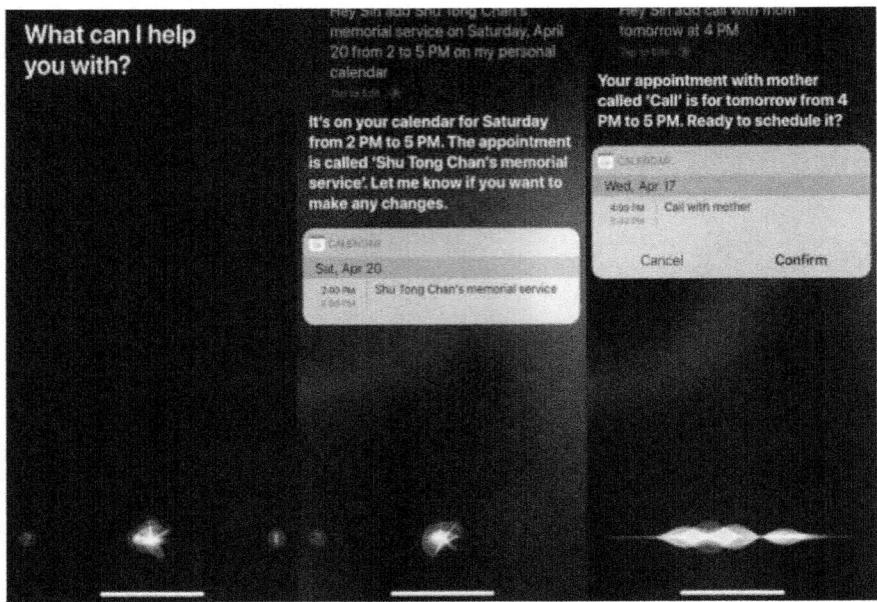

Using Siri to Update a Calendar Event
- Engage Siri with **Home or Power button** or just say **"Hey Siri"**
- Let siri know that you want to move or reschedule an event
- If you have more than one event in a day, siri would ask you to specify the event you want to make changes to
- Next, let siri know the details to be modified
- Siri would ask you for a confirmation after you have given it the new details. You are to reply **Yes** or click the button

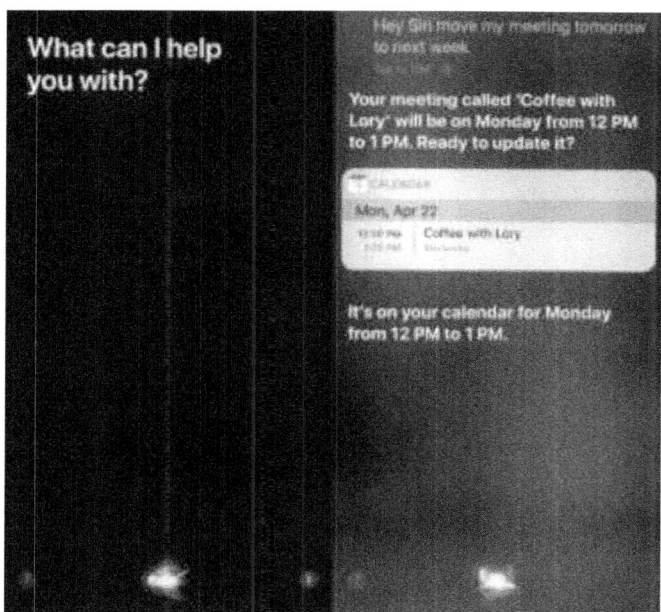

Using Siri to View and Check Your Calendar
- Engage siri with the **Home or Power** button or just say **"Hey Siri"**
- Ask siri something like: "what's my schedule like for today"
- Siri would now reply to your inquiry and read them if there are as well as display the event (s)

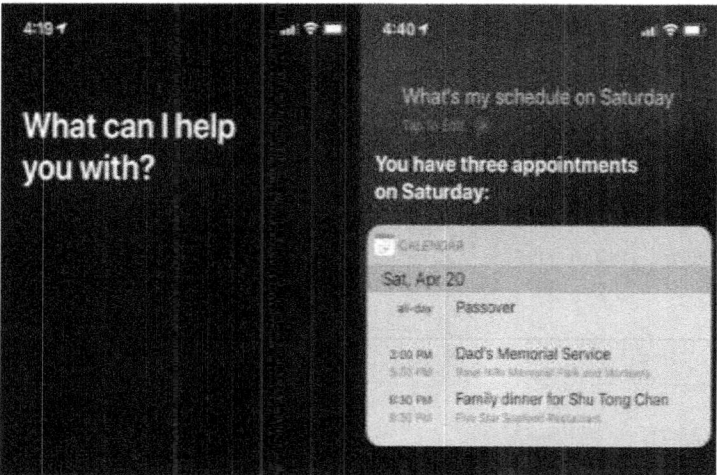

Using Siri to Cancel a Calendar Event

- Engage Siri by pushing and holding the **Home** or **Power button** or say **"Hey Siri"**
- Let siri know the event you want to cancel
- Next, siri would ask for a confirmation of what you just told it. Reply with **Yes**

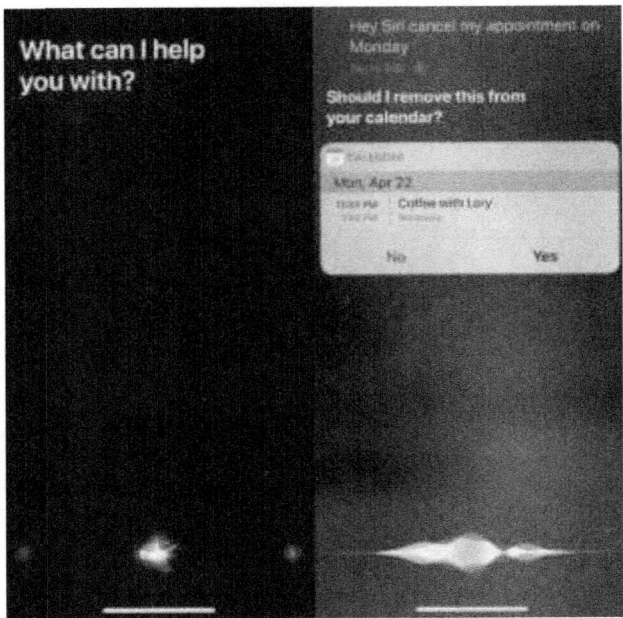

Chapter 18: Maps

With apple maps, you get everything you need to get to where you are going including taking scenic routes and finding interesting places on your way. With Apple Maps, you can know your exact location, the direction you are facing, what's close to you and how to skirt around traffic. There's much more.

Viewing and Sharing Your Current Location
- Click on **Maps**
- Select the **location icon** at top right of the app

Marking Your Current Location
- Click on your **current position** in the Maps app
- Select **Mark My Location**

216

Sharing Your Current Location

- Click on your **current location** in the **Maps** app
- Select **Share My Location**
- Choose **how to share** your position from the choices in the share sheet

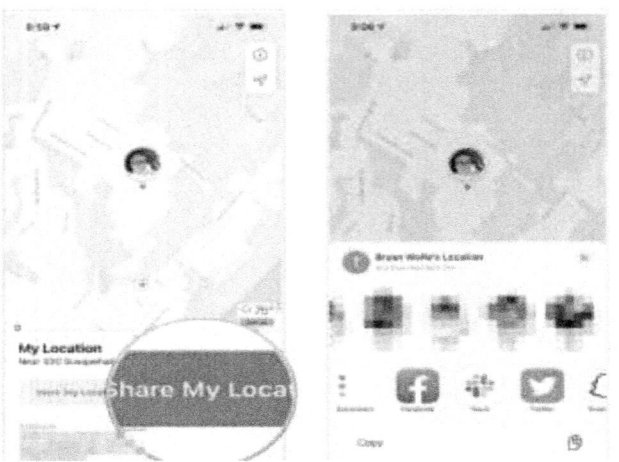

Changing Your Map View

- Click on the **Maps** app
- Locate the **location** you want to map
- Click on the **information** icon at the top right

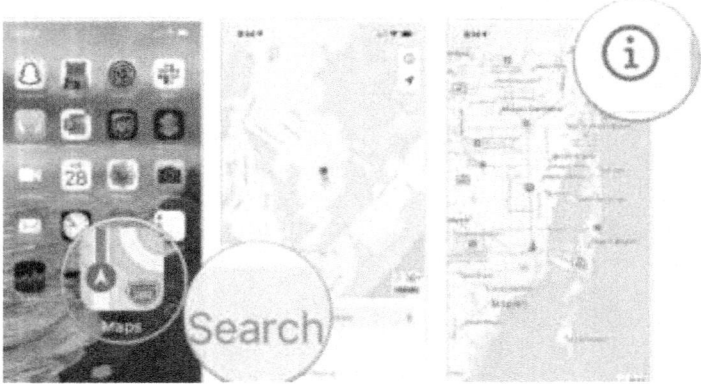

- Select from **Maps, Transit** and **Satellite** as your view

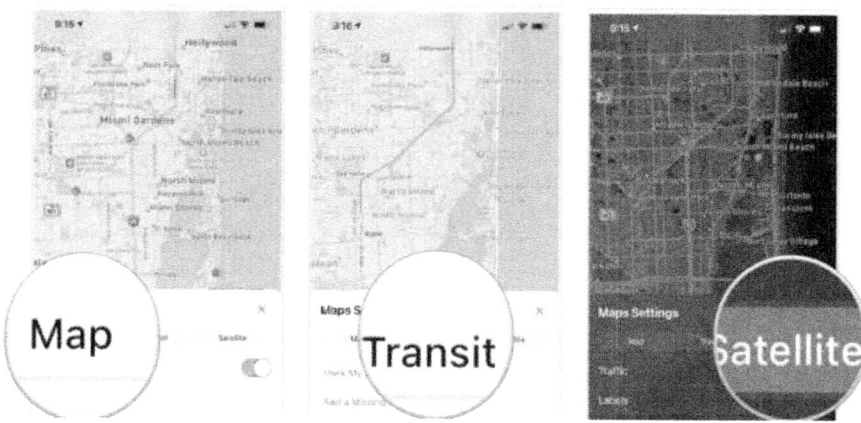

Browsing or Searching a Location

- Click on the **Maps** app
- You can use the **Search box** to locate a place or address

- Click on the **location** to see it on a map
- Select **Directions** to path your trip if needed

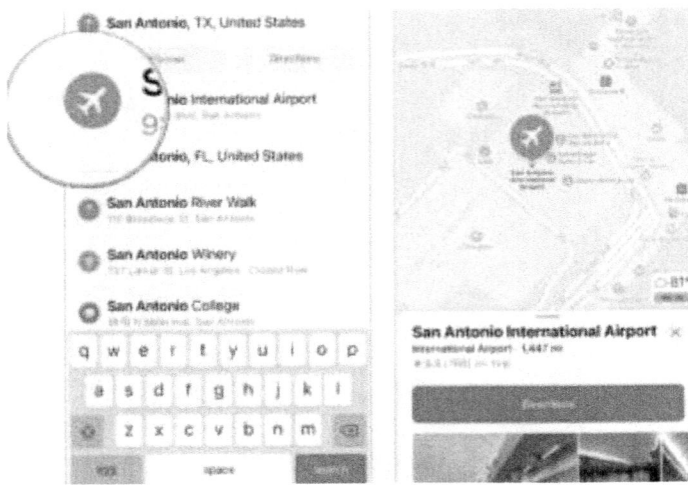

Finding Nearby Locations

- Click on the **Maps** app
- Select the **location icon** at top right of the app so the map would be centered on your location

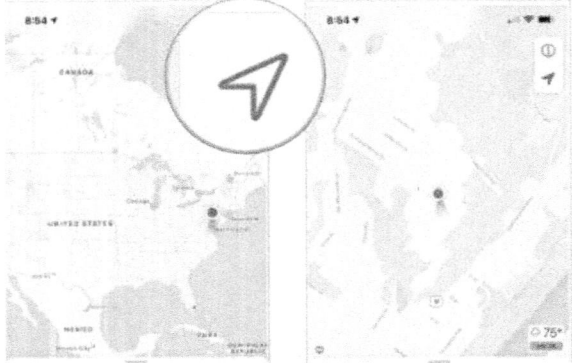

- Select the **Search box**
- Select from the several **categories** under find nearby

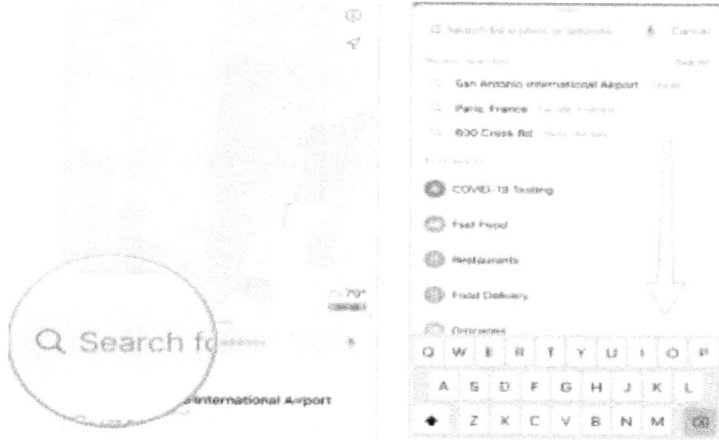

- Click on a **location** found under your chosen category
- Select **Directions** for information on to get to the place from your current position

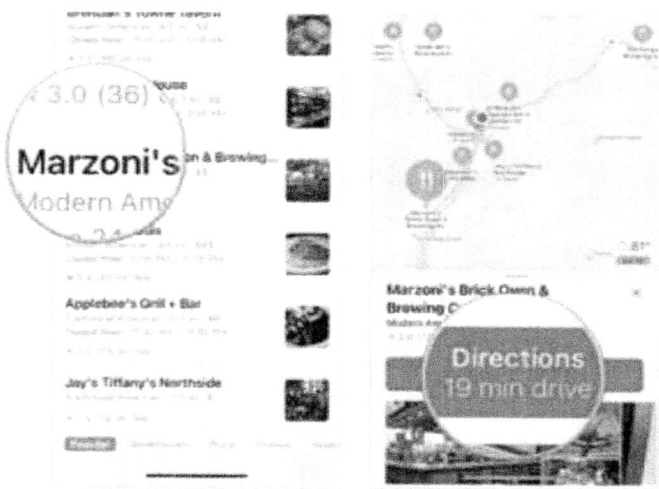

Selecting a Route in Maps
- Click on **Maps**
- With the **Search box,** find a place or address

- Select **Directions** to path the trip

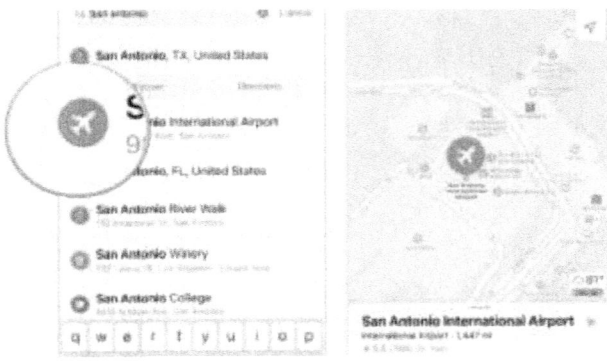

- Choose the **path** on the map that you want to take

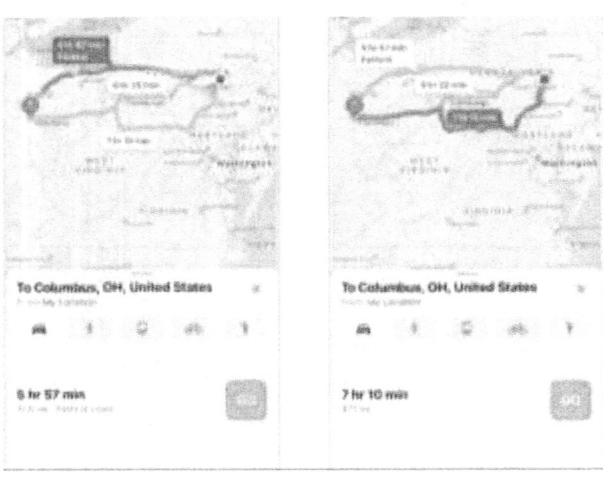

Viewing Recent Map Searches
- Open the **Maps** app
- Click on the **search bar** at screen bottom
- Select the **previous location** on the list

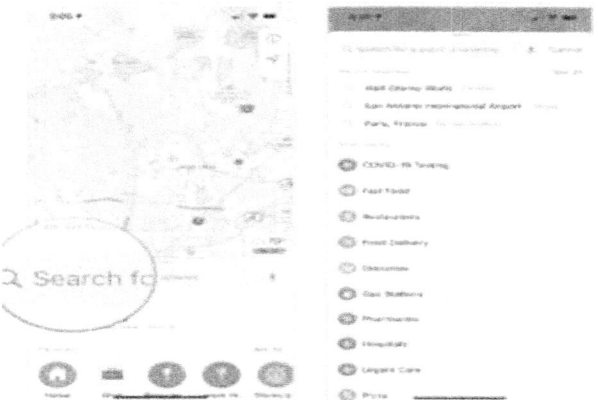

Adding Favorite Locations in Maps
- Open the **Maps** app
- Locate the **location** you want to favorite via the following methods:
- Enter the address in the search bar
- Dropping a pin
- Tapping on a location in the map
- From the **lower panel,** swipe upwards
- Tap on **Add favorite**

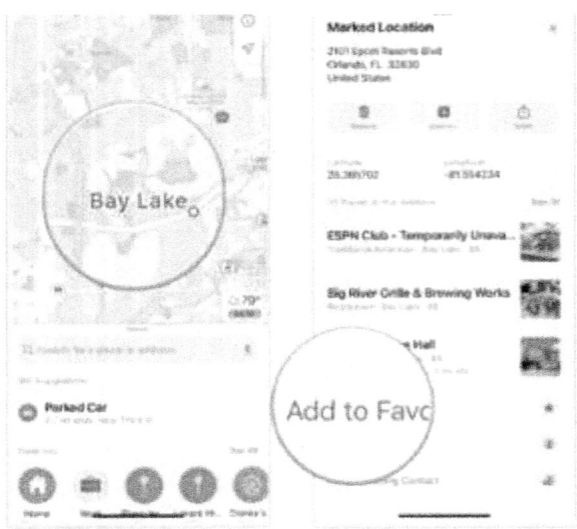

Viewing Favorite Places in Maps
- Open the **Maps app**
- Navigate down and from favorites, tap **See All**

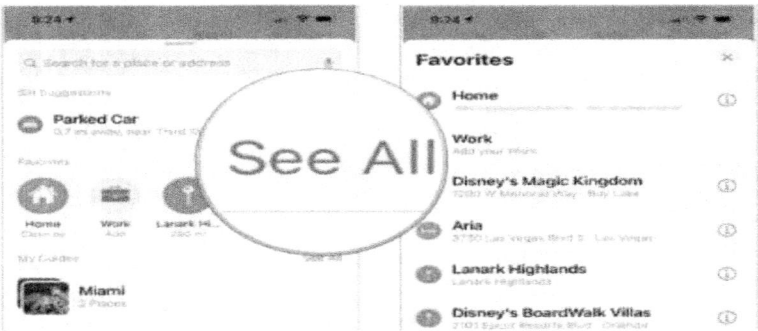

Deleting Favorites from Maps
- Open the **Maps app**
- Navigate down and from favorites, tap **See All**

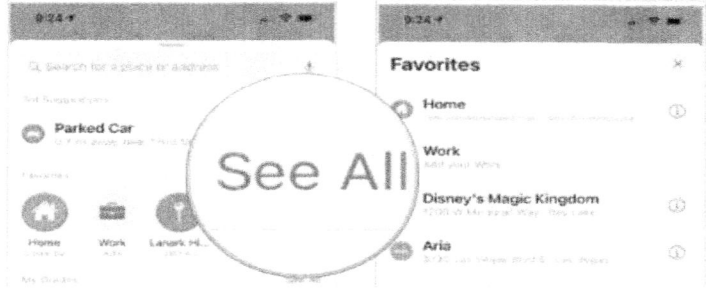

- Navigate to the left on the **location to delete**
- Press **Delete**

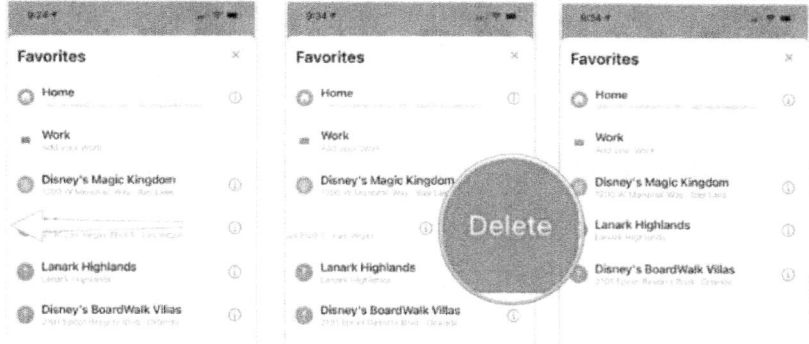

Sharing Directions with Maps

- Open the **Maps** app
- Click the **search bar**
- Type an **address or location**

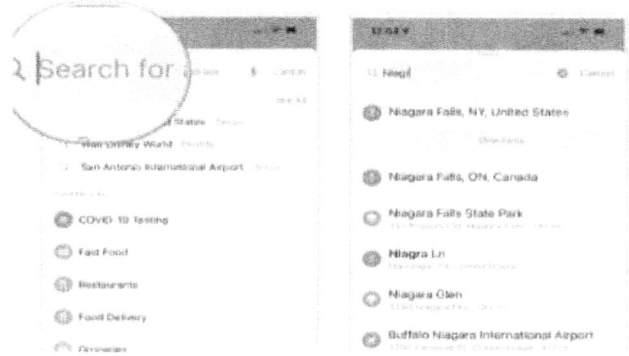

224

- Navigate down and tap the **share sheet icon**
- Next, send via your **preferred medium**

Getting Directions with Siri and Maps
- Activate Siri by saying **"Hey Siri"**
- You can say something like: **"directions to the white house"**
- Next, choose a **mode of transportation.**
- Click **Go** to begin navigation immediately.

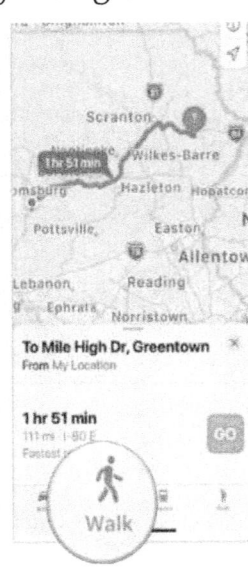
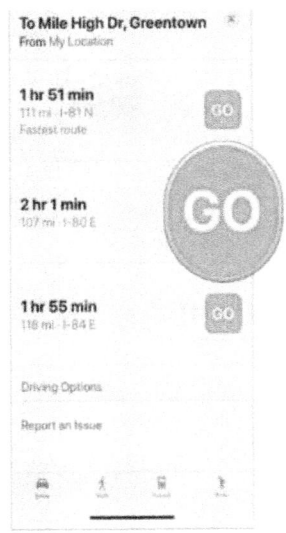

Using Siri and Maps to Locate Local Businesses

- Activate Siri by saying **"Hey Siri"**

- Next, let siri know what you want by saying something like: "directions to the nearest bank"

- Select **your preferred option** in case siri presents more than one

- Click a **mode of transportation** or siri will revert to Drive or Walk based on how close you are to the destination

- Click **Go** to begin the navigation or Siri would start running in a few seconds

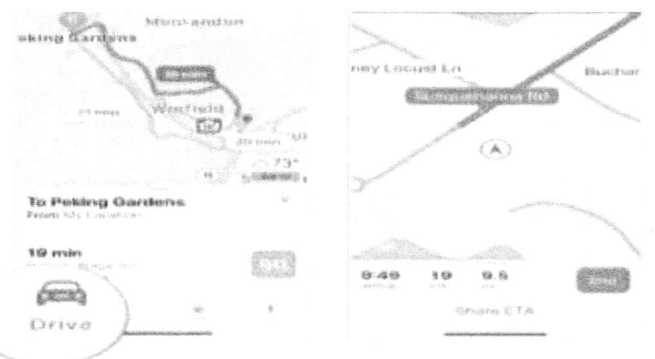

Finding Your Way Home via Siri and Maps

- Activate siri by saying **"Hey Siri"**
- Say: **"take me home"**
- Select a **mode of transportation**
- Click **Start** to begin the navigation or it will automatically do so within a few seconds

To also enable location services:

- Go to **Settings**
- Go to **Privacy**
- Go to **Location Services**

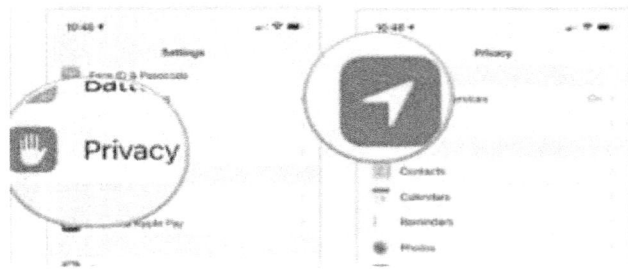

- Click **Maps**
- Select **While Using The App** from Allow Location Access

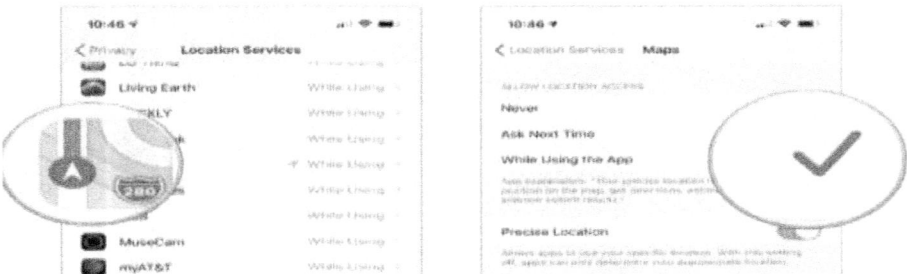

You also need to engage Significant Locations. Follow these steps:

- Go to **Settings**
- Go to **Privacy**

- Go to **Location Services**

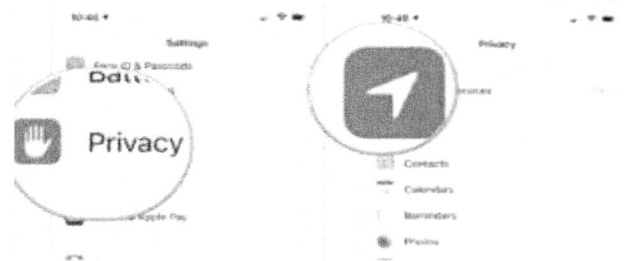

- Navigate down and tap **System Services**
- Switch On **Significant Locations**

Changing the Navigation Voice Volume

- Go to **Settings**
- Click on **Maps**
- Click **Navigation & Guidance**
- Choose the **desired volume level**

Deleting Recent Destination and Search History

- Go to **Maps**
- Swipe **up** to see the **recents** menu
- Swipe to the **left** on a set of directions or a place to call up the **More** menu
- Click **Delete**

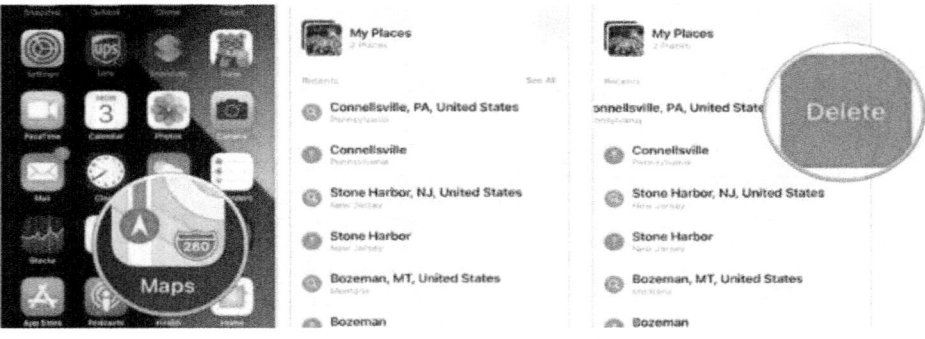

Viewing the Weather in Maps

- Open **Maps**
- Push the **weather button** at lower right corner. There may be a need for you to **zoom in** on the map to make the weather button show up

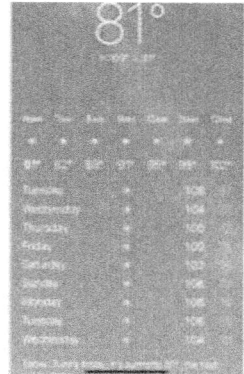

Opening Apple Maps Locations in Google Maps

- Download opener
- Go to **Apple maps**
- Next**, Search** for a location
- **Swipe up** on the information screen to reveal the share button

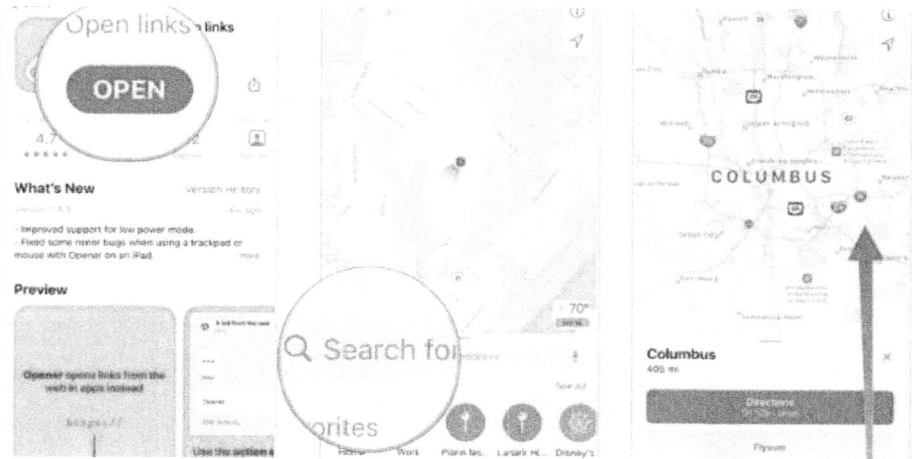

- **Click** the **share button**
- Select **opener**
- Choose the option **Open Link in Google Maps**

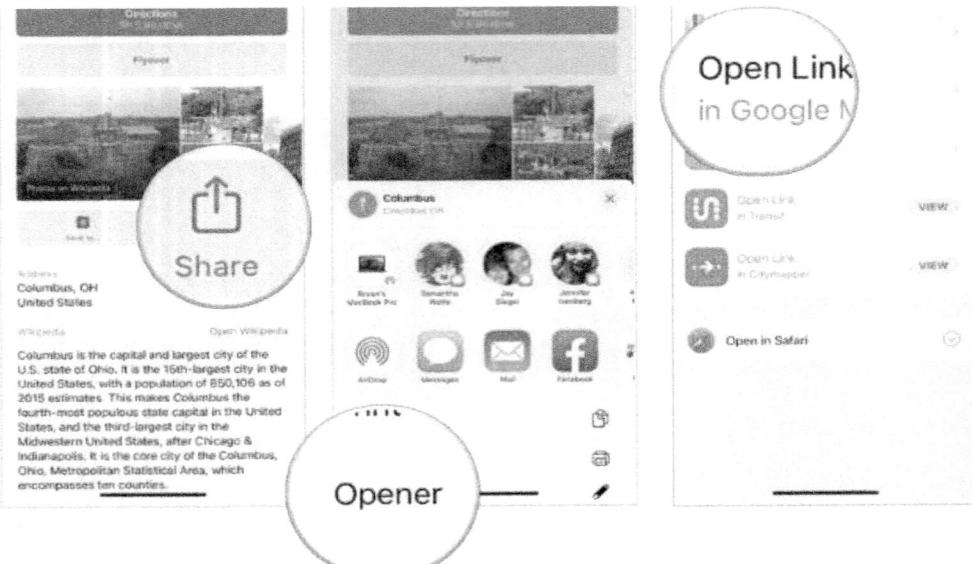

- Click **Open** to affirm that you want to run the directions in Google Maps and Select **Start** in Google Maps to start the journey

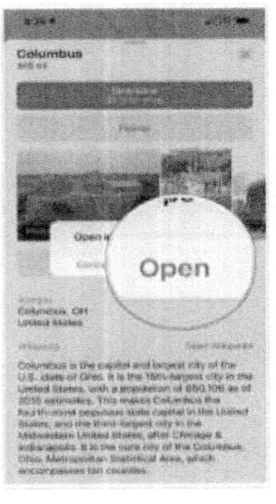  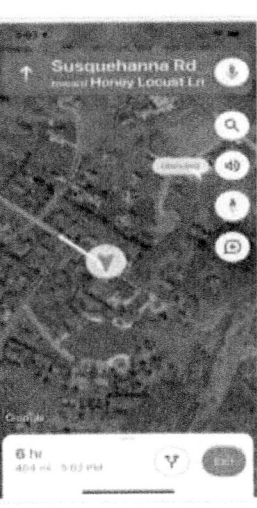

Chapter 19: Podcasts

With Apple podcasts, you can stream and download all your favorite shows and even discover new ones while at it. That's not all. You can still subscribe, sync and customize podcasts to your desire.

Finding, subscribing to and Streaming/downloading Podcasts

- Launch **podcasts**
- Click **Search** in the menu at screen bottom
- Enter the **name** or **genre** of podcast you seek
- Click **Search** at bottom right
- When you find what you seek, **tap** on it
- Click **Subscribe**

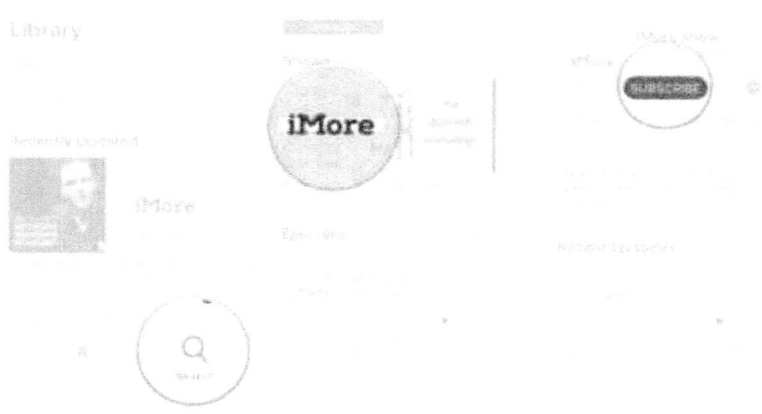

- Click the **download** button next to the episode name.
- Click the **episode** you want to listen to stream it without downloading

Sharing Podcasts and Podcast Episodes

- Open **podcasts**
- Click the **podcast** or click **Details** on the **episode** you want to share. Click the **more** button
- Click **share**
- Click the **method** you want to use to share the podcast or episode. Share normally

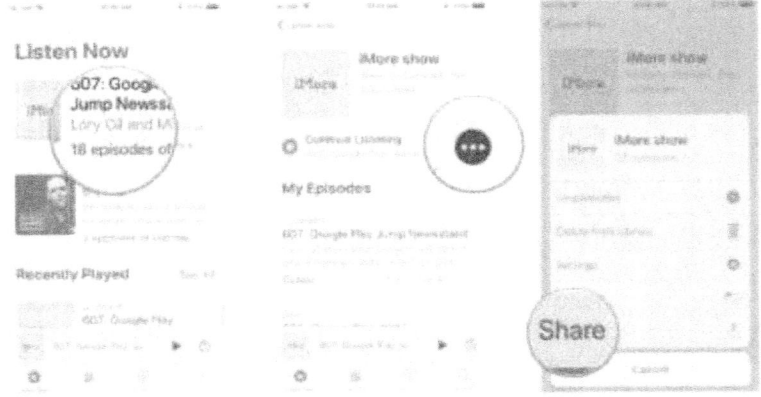

Syncing Podcasts Across Devices

- Go to **Settings.** Click **Podcasts**
- Click the **button** next to **sync Podcasts**

233

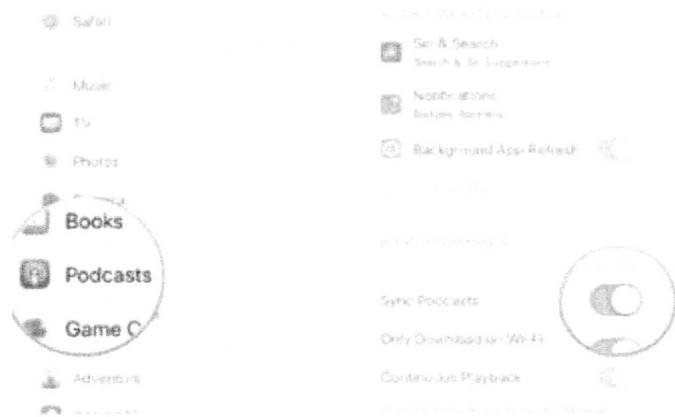

Setting the Refresh Rate for Podcasts
- Go to **Settings.** Click **Podcasts**
- Click **Refresh Every**
- Click **how often** you would want your podcasts to update. Choose between **1 hour, 6 hours, Day, Week, Manually**

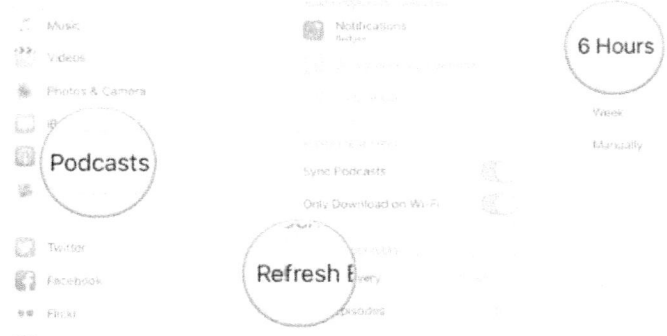

Turning off Delete Played Episodes for Podcasts
- Open **Settings**
- Click **Podcasts**
- Click the **button** next to **Delete Played Episodes** to turn it off

Turning off Notifications for Podcasts
- Open **Settings**
- Click **Podcasts**
- Click **Notifications**

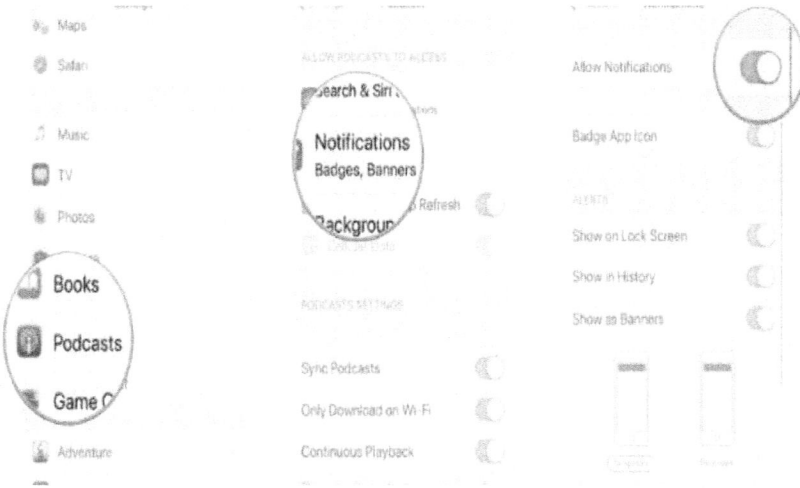

Chapter 20: Find My

This is a feature that combines the functions of Find my iPhone and Find my friends in one app. It's available for iOS 14. Via this app you can share your location with friends and family, view friend locations that has been shared with you. It's also possible for you to track down, remotely lock and wipe lost devices.

Finding Friends in Find My

- Launch **Find My**
- Click on the **People** tab if the app doesn't open to it
- Click the **friend** sharing their location in the list below the map

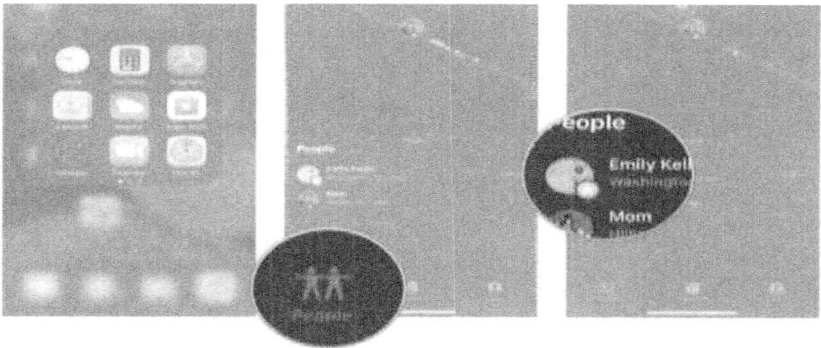

- Next, swipe upwards on the card and click **Contact** to view that friend's contact information
- Click **Directions** to directed to their location in Maps
- Click **Add (Friend's name) to Favorites**

- Click **Edit Location name**
- Click a **label** to the location for e.g. Home, gym, school etc.
- Click **Add Custom Label** to create a custom label for their location

Sharing your Location
- Launch **Find My**
- Click on the **Me** tab
- Click the button next to **Share My Location**

Notifying Friends of Your Location
- Launch **Find My**
- Click the **People** tab in case the app doesn't open to it
- Click a **friend** who is sharing their location in the list below the map

- Swipe upwards and click **Add…** under **Notifications**
- Click **Notify (friend's name)**
- Choose between **When I arrive** or **When I Leave** depending on the preference

- Click on the **location** the notification will be about
- You can also click **Add Location** to add a new location then the listed one

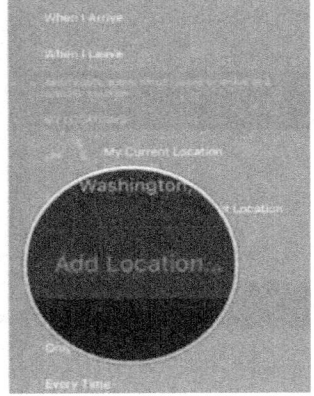

- Choose between **Only Once** or **Every Time** depending on the preference
- Click **Add**

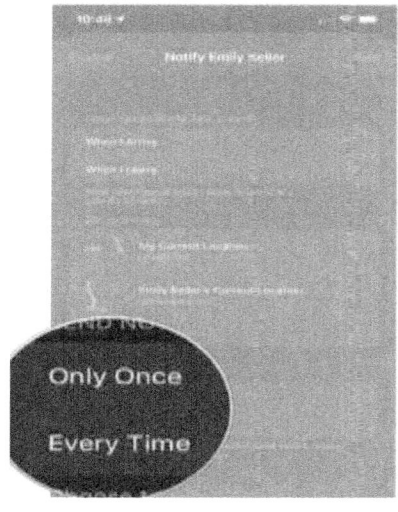 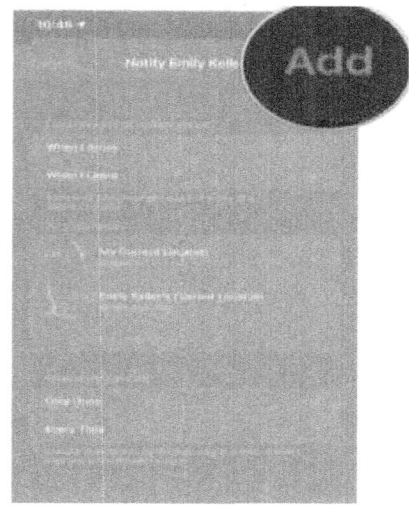

Marking a Device as Lost
- Launch **Find My**
- Click the **Devices** tab and the nearby devices should appear
- Click the device you want to locate

- Swipe upwards and click **Activate** under **Mark as Lost**
- Click **Continue**
- You can choose to **enter your phone number**

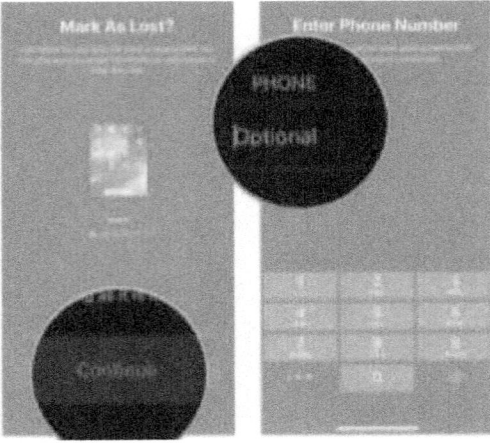

- Click **Next**
- You can **leave a message** for the finder of your device
- Click **Activate**

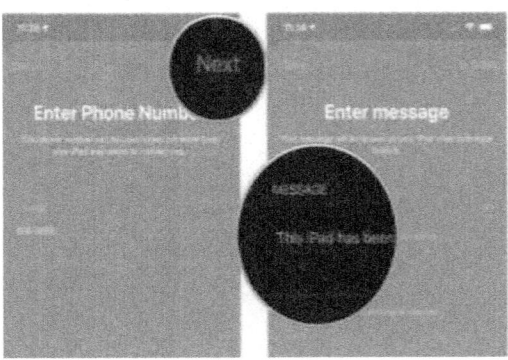

Erasing a Device Remotely
- Launch **Find My**
- Click the **Devices** tab and the nearby ones will show up on the map
- Click the device you want to erase

- Swipe up and click on **Erase This Device**
- Click **Erase This Device**
- You can decide to **enter your phone number**

  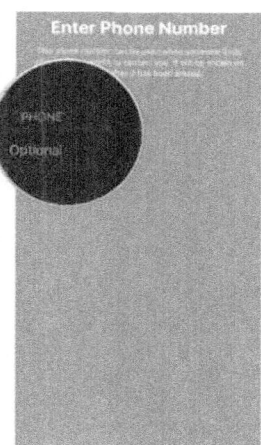

- Click **Next**
- You can decide to **leave a message** for a finder
- Click **Erase**

Managing Your Personal Settings in Find My
- Launch **Find My**
- Click on **Me**
- Swipe up and click the switch close to **Share My Location** to start or stop the sharing of your location

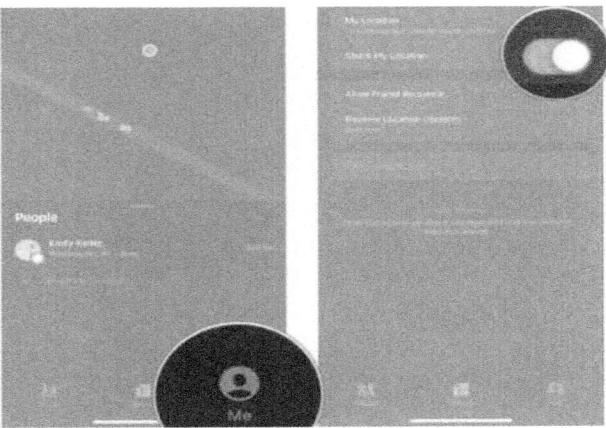

- Click the **switch** next to **Allow Friend Requests**
- Click **Receive Location Updates** to decide who receives updates on your position
- Choose between **people you share with** or **Everyone**

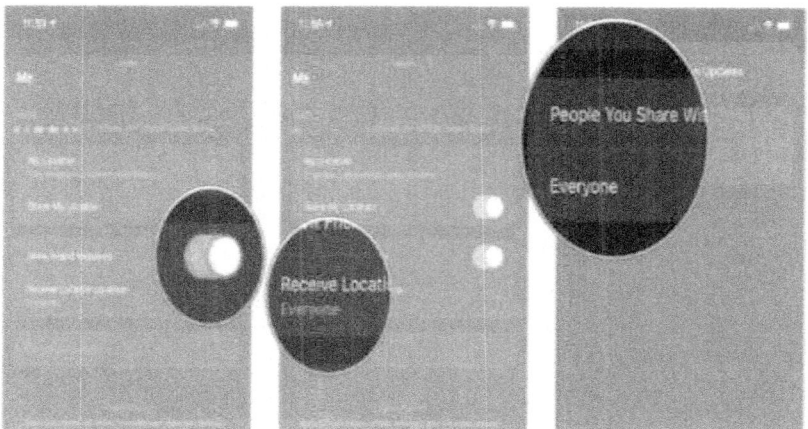

- Click **Me**
- Click **Edit Location Name**
- Click a **label** e.g school, Home, work etc
- click **Add Custom Label** to choose a new custom label for their location

Chapter 21: Face Time

Every apple product has a built in Face Time app. You have the option of doing audio or video calls over a Wi-Fi or cellular data connection. You can stay in touch with family, friends and colleagues even while on the move or traveling. It's very easy to use.

Making a Face Time Audio or Video Call

- Launch **Face Time** on your device

- Click the **+** symbol

- Enter the **name, email address** or **number** you want to call

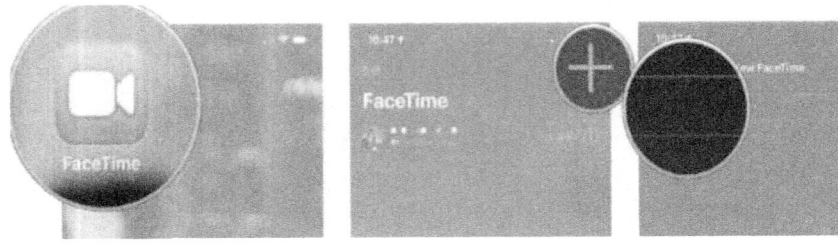

- In case you want to do a group call, you can type more **names, Addresses** or **numbers**

- Click **Audio** or **Video** to begin the call

Making a Group Facetime Call

- From the **FaceTime app**, tap + at top right

- Next, tap the names or numbers of the intended participants in the entry field at top. Tap ⊕ to launch **Contacts** and include people from there
- Tap the **Video** icon to start a video call or tap **Audio** to start a FaceTime audio call

Starting a Group FaceTime Call from a Group Messages Conversation
- From the Messages conversation, tap the **profile pictures** at the top of the conversation
- Next, tap **FaceTime**

Adding a new Person to an existing Call
- From a FaceTime call, **tap the screen** to call up the controls.
- Swipe up from the top of the controls and tap **Add Person**
- Next, type the **name, number or Apple ID** of the person you want to include in the **entry field at top**
- You can also tap + to add someone from your **Contacts**
- Tap **Add Person to FaceTime**
- To exit a Group FaceTime Call, tap ⊗

Switching from a Normal Call to Face Time

- View the **call menu** that shows when you are on a call
- Next, click the Face Time button to begin a Face Time video call

 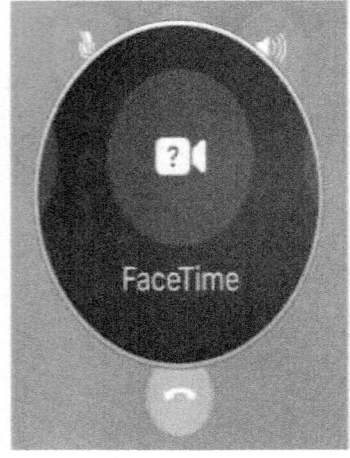

Turning off Video from a Face Time Call

- **Initiate** or **take** a Face Time call
- Push the **Home Button** or **swipe up** from screen bottom depending on your device and the video feed will be put on hold but the other party would still hear you

Using Siri to Place a Face Time Call
- Push and hold the **Home button** or the **Side button** or say "**Hey Siri**" to engage the voice assistant
- Say **"Face Time + (name)** or say **"Face Time"** and wait for Siri's prompt before speaking the name of the person you want to call. Siri would now initiate the call

Using Face Time with Apple TV
- **Swipe upwards** from screen bottom or swipe down on right corner of Home screen depending on device
- Click **Screen Mirroring**
- Click on the device to which you want to mirror your device's screen

Printed in Great Britain
by Amazon